1996–97 Annual Supplement to

THE PIANO BOOK

BUYING & OWNING A NEW OR USED PIANO

LARRY FINE

BROOKSIDE PRESS • BOSTON, MASSACHUSETTS

Brookside Press
P.O. Box 178, Jamaica Plain, Massachusetts 02130
(617) 522-7182
(800) 545-2022 (orders)

e-mail: pianobk@tiac.net
world wide web: http://www.tiac.net/users/pianobk

ISBN 0-9617512-7-4

NOTICE

Reasonable efforts have been made to secure accurate information for this publication. Due
in part to the fact that manufacturers and distributors will not always willingly make this
information available, however, some indirect sources have been relied upon.

Neither the author nor publisher make any guarantees with respect to the accuracy of the
information contained herein and will not be liable for damages—incidental, consequential,
or otherwise—resulting from the use of the information.

INTRODUCTION

This is the first issue of what I expect to be an annual publication, published each year in August. The long span of time between successive editions of *The Piano Book* makes it impractical to provide detailed model and price information in the book itself, information which is increasingly sought by price-conscious consumers. Likewise, manufacturer and product updates are needed on a timely basis to alert consumers to changes that may affect their purchasing decisions. It is hoped that this modest companion volume will effectively extend the "shelf life" of *The Piano Book* as a valuable reference work, as well as serve as an additional information resource for piano buyers and piano lovers.

L.F.

CONTENTS

MANUFACTURER and PRODUCT UPDATE

This section contains piano manufacturer and product changes that have occurred since the third edition of *The Piano Book* went to press in late 1994. It is not intended, however, that this information take the place of the reviews in the book. With some exceptions, this update is limited to changes of a factual nature only, whereas the book contains, in addition, critical reviews and recommendations. If a company or brand name is not listed here, it means that there is nothing new to report. To correctly understand price and model information listed here, please see page 72 of *The Piano Book*.

August Förster

See "Förster, August"

Baldorr & Son

No longer being sold.

Baldwin

At the time the third edition of *The Piano Book* was going to press, Baldwin was in the process of completely reorganizing its product line (and also undergoing major changes in management). The description of the new models given in the book was based on Baldwin's tentative plans at that time, but the plans changed and the actual product line turned out a little differently.

Baldwin also owns the **Wurlitzer** and **Chickering** trade names. In its reorganized product line, the Wurlitzers represent the lower-priced pianos, the Chickerings the mid-priced American-made grands, and the Baldwins the mid- to upper-level verticals and high-end grands. All are sold by the same dealer network. (In the past, Wurlitzer and Baldwin/Chickering had separate dealer networks, and the Baldwin line included instruments at all price levels, which tended to confuse customers about the relative value of the Baldwin name.)

In the new Baldwin line, the spinet model has been discontinued. The console, 43-1/2" in height, comes in three basic model types. All three use the same back and action, but differ in cabinetry. The model E100 is the console with a continental-style cabinet. It has a slightly longer key length and deeper cabinet than the continental-style model it replaces. The model 660 series console is a furniture-style model known as the "Classic". However, unlike the lesser "Classic" model it replaces, this one has Baldwin's 19-ply pinblock, full-size action, and solid spruce soundboard. The upper-level console, the model 2090 series, is called the "Acrosonic", a name Baldwin has traditionally used for its upper-level consoles and spinets. This model series has fancier cabinet features and hardware than the Classic, but is the same instrument inside.

Baldwin 45" studio verticals, still known as the "Hamilton", come in three model types. The model 243HPA is the school studio. Its functional-looking cabinet has been redesigned to provide easier access for servicing, as well as for other practical reasons. The model 5050 series studio, known as the "Limited Edition", is the fancy-looking studio. It is made in only three furniture styles, each limited to a production run of one thousand instruments, after which the style is changed. The model E250 is the studio in a contemporary cabinet style. The 52" "Concert Vertical" upright remains the same.

The Baldwin "Artist" series of grand pianos remains substantially the same, with the following small changes: each piano now comes with an adjustable Artist bench; the sharps are now made of solid ebony wood instead of plastic; the weight characteristics of the action have been changed to reduce inertia; and a 5' 8" Louis XVI style (model 227) has been added to the line.

The Chickering line of American-made grands is new. The two models, 4' 10" (model 410) and 5' 7" (model 507), are adapted from the troublesome Classic line of Baldwin grands that was discontinued at the end of 1994. According to Baldwin, the new models have been redesigned and structurally enhanced.

The Wurlitzer vertical piano line is now limited to a 37" spinet and an entry-level 42" console with a compressed action. All other Wurlitzer consoles, studios, and uprights, both American-made and Korean-made, have been discontinued, since they would otherwise compete with the Baldwin line. The Wurlitzer 5' grand (model G550) and all Wurlitzer grands made by Young Chang have been discontinued. All grands with the Wurlitzer name are now made by Samick (4' 7", 5' 1", and 5' 7") and are the same as the grands formerly bearing the name "D.H. Baldwin", a name which is no longer being used.

Bechner

No longer being sold under this name.

Bechstein, C.

Importation of the W. Hoffmann line of pianos has been discontinued.

Becker, J.

New importer/distributor:

Bellville & Sons
115 Bellam Blvd.
San Rafael, CA 94901

415-456-5314
800-825-1447

Belarus

No longer being distributed here.

Boston

A 5' 1" grand has been added to the line.

Chickering

See "Baldwin"

Disklavier

See "Yamaha"

Dobbert, Fritz (new listing)

Bellville & Sons
115 Bellam Blvd.
San Rafael, CA 94901

415-456-5314
800-825-1447

These pianos are manufactured in Brazil and made their debut in the U.S. a couple of years ago.

Estonia

A 5' 4" grand model, with a Schwander action, has been added to the line. The 6' 3" grand is available with a Renner action, in addition to the standard model with a Schwander action.

Falcone

See "Mason & Hamlin"

Fandrich & Sons (new listing)

Fandrich & Sons Pianos
12515 Lake City Way, NE
Seattle, WA 98125

206-361-1221

Fandrich & Sons pianos are sold by the people who invented the Fandrich Vertical Action. (Note that there is no connection between this company and the Fandrich Piano Company, which uses the Fandrich action in its Fandrich pianos.) Fandrich & Sons pianos, except for the action, are made in China by the Guangzhou Piano Manufactory, the same company that makes Pearl River and Hastings pianos. Fandrich & Sons makes extensive modifications and improvements to the piano in the U.S. and then installs the Fandrich Vertical Action, assembled in the U.S. from parts made by Renner in Germany. The piano is also available with a standard action. At present, these pianos are sold primarily in the Seattle area.

Price range: With Fandrich action — $7,000–8,500; with standard action — $3,800–4,700

Warranty: Twelve years, parts and labor

Models: 46" studio, 51" upright

Feurich

New importer/distributor:

Schimmel Piano Corp.
251 Memorial Drive
Lititz, PA 17543

800-426-3205

Förster, August

New importer/distributor address:

German American Trading Co.
13540 N. Florida Ave.
Tampa, FL 33613

813-961-8405

Fritz Dobbert

See "Dobbert, Fritz"

Grotrian

New importer/distributor:

Strings Limited
314 S. Milwaukee Ave., Ste. B
Libertyville, IL 60048

847-367-5224

Hoffmann, W.

Bechstein has discontinued importing this line of pianos.

Ibach

Soon after the third edition of *The Piano Book* went to press, Daewoo decided not to distribute Korean-made Ibach pianos in the U.S.

Jasper (-American)

See "Kimball"

Kawai

Kawai has replaced its entire KG and GS series of grands with a new RX series. According to the company, these new pianos have "Neotex" keytops (Kawai's brand of ivory substitute), new case beam and plate strut configurations, a non-scratch music desk, and new scale designs. At this time, the prices are about the same as those of the models they replace. Note that the RX-2, which replaces the popular KG-2A, is also available in the variant model RX-2S which, according to the company, is a mellower version of the RX-2, perhaps more suitable for classical music. The only difference between the RX-2 and RX-2S is the hammers. The RX-2S hammers are softer and have heavier maple moldings, resulting in a mellower tone, whereas the RX-2 hammers have the lighter mahogany moldings, as do the rest of the RX series. It's possible that the RX-2 could be voiced to produce a similar effect. [Note: For unknown reasons, the RX-2S does not appear on Kawai price lists.]

The 5' 9" model GE-3 grand replaces the 5' 7" GE-2.

In the verticals, the 44" model 603 replaces the 42" model 602. In the past, the 600 series pianos were technically identical to the 500 series except for cabinetry. However, the new model 603 is larger than the 500 series pianos and has an entirely different scale design.

Kimball

In February 1996, Kimball announced that it would cease all production of vertical pianos. This completes Kimball's exit from the domestic piano business. In July 1995, Kimball stopped making grands, and for a year or so Kimball verticals were largely built by Baldwin, with only cabinets and final assembly by Kimball. Kimball International's Bösendorfer and Herrburger Brooks divisions are unaffected by this change. Kimball will continue to honor its warranties, and will also continue to build piano cabinets for other makers, such as Samick and Kawai, as it has for some time now. The company sold most of its piano-making equipment to a Chinese piano manufacturer, with whom, reportedly, it hopes to develop a joint venture in the Chinese market.

Knabe

This name is now being used on the pianos formerly sold under the "PianoDisc" label. See "Mason & Hamlin" for details.

Knight

Corrected address and phone:

Alfred Knight Ltd.
154 Clapham Park Road
London SW4 7DE England

(44) 71 978 2444

Lyon & Healy

Lyon & Healy is no longer distributing Grotrian pianos. See "Grotrian".

Mason & Hamlin

New phone number: 508-374-8888

In mid-1994, the Mason & Hamlin Companies ceased production of all Mason & Hamlin, Falcone, and Sohmer pianos, and in January 1995 filed for Chapter 7 (liquidation) bankruptcy. Shortly thereafter, a Boston-based piano rebuilding firm, Premier Pianos, obtained the controlling interest in the company from its former owner and persuaded the Bankruptcy Court to change the bankruptcy filing to Chapter 11 (reorganization).

From early 1995 to early 1996, the new owners completed the manufacture of pianos left unfinished when the plant closed, made some new pianos from scratch, and attempted to fight off legal attempts by creditors to force liquidation of the company or its sale to another party. (Many creditors did not have faith in the new owners' ability to put the company back on its feet.) On April 5, 1996, the Court sided with the creditors and approved the sale of Mason & Hamlin to Kirk and Gary Burgett, owners of Music Systems Research, manufacturer of the PianoDisc electronic player piano systems.

At the time of this writing, the Burgett brothers have begun to manufacture Mason & Hamlin pianos once again at the Haverhill, Massachusetts factory to, they say, the original high standards. They will be making the 50" vertical, as well as the models A and BB grands, with initial shipments to dealers planned for late 1996. Some of the instruments will be sold with PianoDisc units installed, but probably most will not. Plans for the Falcone, Sohmer, and George Steck brand names, which were part of the Mason & Hamlin assets, are still being discussed. The Knabe name, also part of the assets, will henceforth be used on the Korean pianos formerly sold under the "PianoDisc" label. The cabinet designs will be changed slightly to reflect the Knabe heritage.

For those who have a need to know, the serial numbers of the Mason & Hamlin pianos built or completed by the interim (Premier) ownership were from 90590 to 90613 inclusive.

Nakamichi / Nakamura

Due to a trademark conflict with the Nakamichi company that sells audio equipment, the Nakamichi piano (no relation) now goes by the name Nakamura.

Pearl River (new listing)

The Piano Group
P.O. Box 49434
Sarasota, FL 34240

800-336-9164
941-953-9628

These pianos are made by Guangzhou Piano Manufactory in Guangzhou, China. This is a return of the Pearl River name, which was used several years ago, but discontinued because the quality of the pianos at that time was not good enough to enable them to maintain a foothold in the U.S. market. The same company makes Hastings pianos, most of which are virtually identical to the Pearl River. According to an informed source, the 46" studio and the 51" upright are the better vertical models in the imported line; the 48" model needs improvement of its design.

Petrof / Weinbach

Petrof now has a 52" upright with a Renner action, not available under the Weinbach label.

The 6' 4" model III Petrof grand (but not Weinbach) now uses Renner action parts, though not a complete Renner action. The parts are assembled onto a Petrof action frame at the Petrof factory. The 7' 9" and 9' 3" models have complete Renner actions. However, a new 6' 4" model III-M, made in the same factory as the two larger models, does have a complete Renner action, as well as other refinements common to the larger models.

Petrof has switched from Delignit to a 7-ply beech pinblock in its Petrof and Weinbach grands.

PianoDisc

The parent company is now called Music Systems Research.

The new PianoDisc model PDS 128 Plus incorporates both floppy disk and compact disc drives in the same unit. The sounds for the "Symphony" option are new—the same as the ones in the new QuietTime product.

QuietTime is PianoDisc's new "silent" piano, which, like the PianoDisc, is retrofittable into any piano. QuietTime turns a piano into a hybrid acoustic/digital instrument. In regular mode, the piano plays just like an ordinary piano. When the QuietTime feature is activated, the acoustic sound is turned off (the hammers are prevented from hitting the strings) and the digital piano (and other instrumental) sounds are turned on. It's MIDI-compatible, of course, and can even be combined with a PianoDisc system. A headphone jack is supplied for private listening. QuietTime's installed price is around $1,795.

The piano formerly called "PianoDisc" is now called "Knabe". It is still made by Young Chang. See "Mason & Hamlin".

QRS / Pianomation

This company now makes a version of Pianomation called "Playola", which sits atop the keys (like the "Vorsetzer" of the player piano's halcyon days) and plays the keys with little rubber fingers, either alone or accompanied by orchestral sounds. Unlike Pianomation, the Playola does not operate the pedals. Instead, quasi-pedal ("Magic Pedal") information is incorporated into the software and simulates the pedals through the control of note duration. This simulation is not as realistic as actually controlling the damper pedal, but should probably be sufficient for simpler applications. Playola comes with a carrying case and does not require professional installation by a technician.

Rieger-Kloss

New importer/distributor:

Weber Piano Co.
40 Seaview Drive
Secaucus, NJ 07094

201-902-0920

Rieger-Kloss now has a 6' 1" grand piano (model 185). Its case and plate are made in Korea by Young Chang, identical to Young Chang's own grand of the same size. The action is made in Germany by Renner and everything else in the piano is made in the Czech Republic. Rieger-Kloss verticals still use mostly Czech components.

Samick

Samick has added Kluge keys, Renner actions, and Abel hammers to its four largest grand piano models (6' 1", 6' 8", 7' 4", 9' 1") and has designated them as its "World Piano" series. According to the company, these models also receive extra pre-sale preparation in the U.S. before being shipped to dealers. In Samick's Kohler & Campbell line, the 6' 10" and 7' models are "World Pianos," though only the 7' has the full complement of features. The 6' 10" grand uses Samick keys, Renner action, and Renner hammers.

Samick has added a 4' 11" grand model SG-150, discontinued its 5' 1" model, and replaced it with a 5' 3-1/2" model SG-161. The 5' 1" model remains, however, in the Kohler & Campbell line.

Sängler & Söhne

New importer/distributor address:

North American Music
126 Rt. 303
W. Nyack, NY 10994

914-353-3520
800-541-2331

Schimmel

Schimmel will soon discontinue selling its 5' 1" grand.

Schubert (new listing)

Tri-Con Music Group
1626 North Prospect Ave. #2006
Milwaukee, WI 43202

941-953-9628
800-336-9164

These pianos are made by the Chernikov piano factory in the Ukraine.

Seiler

Seiler's 48" and 52" uprights now come equipped with the optional "Super Magnet Repetition" (SMR) action, a patented feature that uses magnets to increase repetition speed. Tiny magnets are attached to certain action parts of each note. During playing, the magnets repel each other, forcing the parts to return to their rest position faster, ready for a new key stroke. These instruments will be priced about the same as the regular models.

Sohmer

See "Mason & Hamlin"

Steinway & Sons

In April 1995, Steinway Musical Properties, Inc., parent corporation of Steinway & Sons, was purchased by Selmer Industries, Inc., parent corporation of The Selmer Company, a major manufacturer of band instruments. The new combined company, to be known as Steinway Musical Instruments, Inc., is now in the process of conducting a public stock offering. Management at Steinway & Sons remains the same.

It is well known that a principal competition to Steinway pianos comes from used and rebuilt Steinways. Steinway has responded by reissuing old, turn-of-the-century designs, available in models L (5' 10-1/2") and B (6' 10-1/2"), in ebony and rosewood. These models, known as "Instruments of the Immortals", are priced about $5,000-9,000 higher than the regular models of the same finish. The new/old designs are actually an amalgam of several different period designs, and include: round, "ice-cream cone" legs; elaborately carved music desk; distinctive arm profile and lyre designs; raised bead on case and around plate holes; and fancy, old soundboard and fallboard decals, among other features. The pianos come with matching bench.

Steinway has released a computer CD called "An Interactive Factory Tour" containing more than one hundred photos and video clips illustrating how its instruments are made. To obtain a copy, call or visit your local Steinway dealer. Technicians can buy it from the Steinway Parts Dept.

Story & Clark

Story & Clark now makes a 5' 5" grand (the "Hampton") in the U.S. It is unusual in that its maple rim is made in four pieces, which are glued and doweled together, rather than being one continuous rim bent around a form like most other grand rims. The piano has German Abel hammers with a Czech-made action, and comes in several different furniture styles.

This summer, a new 44" console ("Prelude") is being introduced, made in China by the Dongbei Piano Co. On some models, Story & Clark will assemble the action and cabinet onto a Chinese strung back. Later in the year, Story & Clark will introduce a 5' 4" grand made by Estonia with the Story & Clark name on it.

Weinbach

See "Petrof/Weinbach"

Wieler

See "Sängler & Söhne"

Woodchester (new listing)

The Woodchester Piano Co. Ltd.
Woodchester Mills
Woodchester, Stroud
Gloucestershire GL5 5NW
England

(44) 453 872871

This English company was founded in 1994 on the site of the old Bentley piano factory, which was abandoned when Bentley was purchased by another company. Some of the old Bentley workforce continues to work for Woodchester.

Woodchester manufactures vertical pianos from 44-1/2" to 48" in height. The larger models have Renner actions, Abel hammers, Delignit pinblocks, and backs based on a Rippen design. Components for the smaller models are from Poland and the Czech Republic.

Prices range: approximately $4,000-8,000

Warranty: Five years, parts and labor

Wurlitzer

See "Baldwin"

Yamaha

Models G1 and G2 (5' 3" and 5' 8") have been replaced with models C1 and C2 of the same size. As far as I can tell, the change is mostly in name; technically the new models are nearly identical to the old.

Most Yamaha models are now available as Disklaviers, and many are available as "Silent Pianos." The 48" model U1 is currently the only model available as both a Silent Piano and Disklavier in the same piano (model MPX100II). The model GH1B grand comes in both regular Disklavier format and in a format with the playback feature only (model DGH1BXG); an internal tone card supplies orchestral sounds for accompaniment.

Young Chang

Young Chang has new "fashion model" vertical pianos with handsigned prints by Italian artists on the upper front panels. The prints can be ordered separately and fitted to any existing polyester-finish pianos. The price of this feature is about $800.

OTHER TOPICS

Dampp-Chaser Electronics Corp., which manufactures humidity-control equipment for pianos, has introduced several new models and enhancements, including systems that provide humidity control at the back of a vertical piano (where the design of the piano prevents placement of the system inside the front); systems that control humidity at both the back and front, for maximum protection; systems especially designed for climates that are unusually wet or unusually dry; and a "smart" heating element in the humidifier that turns itself off when no water is detected on the cloth pads.

MODEL and PRICING GUIDE

This guide contains the "list price" for nearly every brand, model, style, and finish of new piano that has regular distribution in the United States and, for the most part, Canada. Some marginal, local, or "stencil" brands are omitted. Prices are in U.S. dollars and the pianos are assumed to be for sale in the U.S. (Canadians may find the information useful after translation into Canadian dollars, but there may be differences in import duties and sales practices that will affect retail prices.) Prices and specifications are, of course, subject to change. Most manufacturers raise their prices at least once a year; two or three times a year is not uncommon when international currency values are unstable. The prices in this edition were compiled in the spring of 1996.

Some terms used in this guide require special explanation and disclaimers:

List Price

This is a "standard" list price computed according to a formula commonly used in the industry. The list price is usually a starting point for negotiation, not a final sales price. For their own suggested retail prices, some manufacturers use a different formula, usually one that raises the prices above "standard" list by ten to fifteen percent so that their dealers can advertise a larger "discount" without losing profit. For this reason, price-shopping by comparing discounts from the manufacturer's suggested retail price may result in a faulty price comparison. To provide a level playing field for comparing prices, most prices in this guide are computed according to the same "standard" formula, even though it may differ from the manufacturers' own suggested retail prices. [Exception: Some Steinway suggested retail prices are *lower* than "standard" list, but I'm using Steinway's prices in this guide because in many cases they are close to the actual selling prices, and comparison shopping is not as big an issue as it is with other brands.] For most models, the price includes a bench and the standard manufacturer's warranty for that brand (see *The Piano Book* for details). Most dealers will also include moving and one or two tunings in the home, but these are optional and a matter of agreement between you and the dealer.

Style and Finish

Unless otherwise indicated, the cabinet style is assumed to be "traditional" and is not stated. Exactly what "traditional" means varies from brand to brand. In general, it is a "classic" styling with minimal embellishment and straight legs. The vertical pianos have front legs, which are free-standing on smaller verticals and attached to the cabinet with toe blocks on larger verticals. "Continental" or European styling refers to vertical pianos without front legs or decorative trim. Other furniture styles (Chippendale, French Provincial, Queen Anne, etc.) are as noted. The manufacturer's own trademarked style name is used when an appropriate generic name could not be determined.

Unless otherwise stated, all finishes are assumed to be "satin", which reflects light but not images. "Polished" finishes, also known as "high-gloss" or "high-polish", are mirror-like. "Oiled" finishes are usually matte (not shiny). "Ebony" is a black finish.

Special-order–only styles and finishes are in italics.

Some descriptions of style and finish may be slightly different from the manufacturer's own for the purpose of clarity, consistency, saving space, or other reason.

Size

The height of a vertical piano is measured from the floor to the top of the piano. The length of a grand piano is measured from the very front (keyboard end) to the very back (tail end).

About Actual Selling or "Street" Prices

Buying a piano is something like buying a car—the list price is deliberately set high in anticipation of negotiating.[*] But sometimes this is carried to extremes, as when the salesperson reduces the price three times in the first fifteen minutes to barely half the sticker price. In situations like this, the customer, understandably confused, is bound to ask in exasperation, "What is the *real* price of this piano?"

Unfortunately, there *is* no "real" price. In theory, the dealer pays a wholesale price and then marks it up by an amount sufficient to cover the overhead and produce a profit. In practice, however, the markup can vary considerably from sale to sale depending on such factors as:

---

[*] A relatively small number of dealers have non-negotiable prices.

- how long the inventory has been sitting around, racking up finance charges for the dealer

- the dealer's cash flow situation

- the competition in that particular geographic area for a particular brand or type of piano

- special piano sales events taking place in the area

- how the salesperson sizes up your situation and your willingness to pay

- the level of pre- and post-sale service the dealer seeks to provide

- the dealer's other overhead expenses

It's not unusual for one person to pay fifty percent more than another for the same brand and model of piano—sometimes even from the same dealer on the same day! It may seem as if pricing is so chaotic that no advice can be given, but in truth, enough piano sales do fall within a certain range of typical profit margins that some guidance is possible as long as the reader understands the limitations inherent in this kind of endeavor.

Historically, discounts from "standard" list price have averaged ten or fifteen percent in the piano business. In recent years, however, conditions have changed such that, according to some industry sources, the average discount from list has increased to twenty or twenty-five percent. Essentially, due to growing competition from used pianos and digital pianos, and a decrease in the cultural importance attached to having a piano in the home, there are too many dealers of new pianos chasing after too few consumer dollars. In addition, higher labor costs worldwide and unfavorable international currency values make some brands so expensive in the U.S. that they can only be sold at very large discounts. I think, too, that consumers are becoming more savvy and are shopping around. Unfortunately, the overhead costs of running a traditional piano store are so high that most dealers cannot stay in business if they sell at an average discount from list price of more than about twenty percent. To survive, dealers are evolving multiple new approaches: becoming more efficient, instituting low-price/high volume strategies, cutting their overhead—sometimes including service—or subsidizing their meager sales of new pianos with used pianos (which command higher profit margins), rentals, rebuilding, and other products and services.

Although the average discount has increased, it is by no means uniform. Some brands dependably bring top dollar; others languish or the price is highly situational. I did consider giving a typical range of "street" prices for each brand and model listed in this volume, but decided that the task would be too daunting due to the extreme variation in price that can exist from one situation to another, as well as the political fallout that would likely result from dealers and manufacturers who fear the loss of what little power they still have over aggressive, price-shopping customers. To prevent excessive unpleasantness, I have resigned myself for now to just giving general advice in print. (For those who desire more specific information on "street" prices, I offer additional services, such as private telephone consultations and a Pricing Guide Service on the World Wide Web.)

It should be clearly understood that the advice given here is based on my own observations, subjective judgment, and general understanding of the piano market, *not* on statistical sales data or scientific analysis. (Brand-by-brand statistical sales data are virtually nonexistent.) This knowledge is the product of discussions with hundreds of customers, dealers, technicians, and industry executives over the years. Other industry observers may come to different conclusions. This rundown of "street" prices won't cover every brand, but should give a rough idea of what to expect and the ability to predict prices for some of the brands not specifically covered. I can't emphasize enough, however, that pricing can be highly situational, dependent on the mix of available products and the ease of comparison shopping in any particular geographic area, as well as on the financial situation of dealer and customer. The following generalizations should prove useful to you, but expect almost anything.

As a general rule of thumb:

- the more expensive the piano, the higher the possible discount

- the more "exclusive" a brand is perceived to be, the less likely head-to-head competition, and therefore the lower the possible discount

- the longer a piano remains unsold, the higher the possible discount

- the more service-intensive the piano, the lower the possible discount

Japanese and Korean brands are often perceived as being in direct competition with each other, as well as with those of the same national origin. Although discounts from "standard" list price on Japanese and Korean pianos typically start at perhaps fifteen percent, twenty or even thirty percent is not uncommon on the more expensive models or in a moderately competitive environment, especially if the dealer knows the customer is shopping around. Japanese pianos may be especially prone to deep discounting at times because they are less service-intensive than other brands (a testament to the perfection of their manufacturing processes) and because unfavorable currency values and higher labor costs make them relatively expensive. American-made pianos by Japanese companies are less expensive and probably less prone to deep discounting.

Korean pianos have the disadvantage of having too many different brand names made by the same two companies. When several of these are found in the same market, it tends to drive prices down. In addition, since Korean pianos are often the least expensive instruments in a dealer's inventory, the dealer may choose to sell one at a very low price to fit a very limited budget. Most dealers would rather sell you *something*, even at relatively little profit, than turn you away. For this reason, entry-level Korean grands in particular can be amazingly affordable.

The Boston piano, although manufactured in Japan, is generally viewed as being a little more exclusive due to its association with Steinway, so deep discounting is much less likely. The same principle holds true for Baldwin, whose pianos are usually seen as being distinctly different from the Asian products even though they often share common price ranges. Baldwin also benefits from exceptional name recognition and its historical "made in USA" connection. For both brands, discounting is likely to be moderate, in my experience.

Western European instruments tend to be extremely expensive here due to their high quality, the high European cost of doing business, and unfavorable exchange rates. There appear to be two types of dealers of these pianos. One type, usually specializing in selling higher-quality instruments to a demanding clientele, manages to get top dollar for them despite their high price, with discounts averaging only ten to twenty percent. They are not particularly into negotiating. The other type of dealer, probably more numerous, depends for his or her "bread and butter" on consumer-grade pianos and is pleased to make a relatively small profit on the occasional sale of a luxury instrument. Discounts here may well approach forty percent at times, especially if the piano has gone unsold for an extended period of time.

At the other end of the price spectrum, most Russian and Chinese pianos are so cheap, and require so much servicing by the dealer, that it's simply not cost-effective to sell them for much less than full list price. Don't expect much in the way of discounts. Eastern European brands like Petrof are already seen as being a good deal for the money, have little in the way of direct competition, and are fairly service-intensive for the dealer, so expect lower than normal discounts off of list price.

Steinway pianos have always been in a class by themselves, historically the only expensive piano to continually command high profit margins. Except for older Steinways and the occasional Mason & Hamlin, Steinway has little competition and only about one hundred dealers in the United States. Service requirements can be quite high, at least in part because of the higher standards often required to satisfy a fussier clientele. Historically, Steinway pianos have sold at or near full manufacturer's suggested retail price. This is still true in many places, but in recent years I have seen a little more discounting than in the past. Ten to twenty percent is not unusual in some areas; as much as twenty-five percent would be rare.

There is no "fair" price for a piano except the one the buyer and seller agree on. The dealer is no more obligated to sell you a piano at a deep discount than you are obligated to pay the list price. Many dealers are simply not able to sell at the low end of the range consistently and still stay in business. It's understandable that you would like to pay the lowest price possible, and there's no harm in asking, but remember that piano shopping is not just about chasing the lowest price. Be sure you are getting the instrument that best suits your needs and preferences and that the dealer is committed to providing the proper pre- and post-sale service.

For more information on shopping for a new piano and on how to save money, please see pages 60–68 in *The Piano Book* (third edition).

Model	Size	Style and Finish	Price*

Astin-Weight

Verticals

375	41"	Ebony	5,964.
375	41"	Spanish Oiled Oak	6,132.
375	41"	Spanish Lacquer Oak	6,228.
375	41"	Italian Oiled Walnut	6,316.
375	41"	Italian Lacquer Walnut	6,360.
375	41"	Regency Oiled Oak	6,316.
375	41"	Regency Lacquer Oak	6,404.
375	41"	Regency Oiled Walnut	6,404.
375	41"	Regency Lacquer Walnut	6,546.
U-500	50"	Ebony	8,282.
U-500	50"	Oiled Oak	8,282.
U-500	50"	Lacquer Oak	8,484.
U-500	50"	Oiled Walnut	8,590.
U-500	50"	Lacquer Walnut	8,722.

Grands

———	5' 9"	Ebony	34,000.

August Förster — see "Förster, August"

Baldwin

Verticals

660	43-1/2"	Mahogany	3,940.
662	43-1/2"	Queen Anne Cherry	3,940.
665	43-1/2"	Country Oak	3,940.
E100	43-1/2"	Continental Mahogany	3,960.
E100	43-1/2"	Continental Polished Ebony	4,150.
E100	43-1/2"	Continental Polished Ivory	4,150.
2090	43-1/2"	Hepplewhite Mahogany	4,650.
2095	43-1/2"	Oak	4,650.
2096	43-1/2"	Queen Anne Cherry	4,650.
243HPA	45"	Ebony	4,780.
243HPA	45"	Golden Oak	4,780.
243HPA	45"	American Walnut	4,780.

*For explanation of terms and prices, please see pages 19–24.

Model	Size	Style and Finish	Price*
Baldwin (continued)			
5050	45"	Mahogany	5,980.
5052	45"	Queen Anne Cherry	5,980.
5057	45"	Queen Anne Oak	5,980.
E250	45"	Contemporary Polished Ebony	5,100.
6000	52"	Ebony	8,590.
6000	52"	Mahogany	8,790.
Grands			
M	5' 2"	Ebony	18,720.
M	5' 2"	Polished Ebony	19,500.
M	5' 2"	Mahogany	19,720.
M	5' 2"	Polished Mahogany	20,520.
R	5' 8"	Ebony	21,320.
R	5' 8"	Polished Ebony	22,100.
R	5' 8"	Mahogany	22,320.
R	5' 8"	Polished Mahogany	23,200.
226	5' 8"	French Provincial Cherry	26,100.
226	5' 8"	French Provincial Polished Cherry	26,800.
227	5' 8"	Louis XVI Ebony	25,800.
227	5' 8"	Louis XVI Mahogany	26,500.
L	6' 3"	Ebony	24,300.
L	6' 3"	Polished Ebony	25,100.
L	6' 3"	Mahogany	25,300.
L	6' 3"	Polished Mahogany	26,200.
SF10	7'	Ebony	36,100.
SF10	7'	Polished Ebony	37,000.
SF10	7'	Mahogany	37,200.
SD10	9'	Ebony	57,900.
Grands–all		*Add for solid color finishes*	2,000.
Grands–all		*Add for veneer change (selected)*	2,800.

Bechstein, C.

Verticals			
110	44"	Polished Ebony	21,030.
110	44"	Rufflelaquer Ebony	21,030.
110	44"	Mahogany	20,360.

Model	Size	Style and Finish	Price*
110	44"	Oak	20,360.
110	44"	Walnut	21,030.
110	44"	Cherry	21,030.
110	44"	Polished White	21,820.
115	45"	Polished Ebony	24,980.
115	45"	Rufflelaquer Ebony	24,980.
115	45"	Mahogany	24,290.
115	45"	Oak	24,290.
115	45"	Walnut	24,980.
115	45"	Cherry	24,980.
115	45"	Polished White	25,750.
12N	45"	Polished Ebony	31,100.
12N	45"	Mahogany	30,100.
12N	45"	Oak	30,100.
12N	45"	Walnut	31,100.
12N	45"	Cherry	31,100.
12N	45"	Polished Woods (above)	32,080.
12N	45"	Polished White	32,080.
12N	45"	Yew	32,080.
12A	46"	Polished Ebony	33,540.
12A	46"	Mahogany	32,580.
12A	46"	Oak	32,580.
12A	46"	Walnut	33,540.
12A	46"	Cherry	33,540.
12A	46"	Polished Woods (above)	34,520.
12A	46"	Polished White	34,520.
12A	46"	Yew	34,520.
120	47"	Polished Ebony	27,100.
120	47"	Rufflelaquer Ebony	27,100.
120	47"	Mahogany	26,420.
120	47"	Oak	26,420.
120	47"	Walnut	27,100.
120	47"	Cherry	27,100.
120	47"	Polished White	27,900.
122	48"	Polished Ebony	28,940.
122	48"	Cherry	28,940.

*For explanation of terms and prices, please see pages 19–24.

Model	Size	Style and Finish	Price*

Bechstein, C. (continued)

Model	Size	Style and Finish	Price*
11A	48"	Polished Ebony	38,220.
11A	48"	Mahogany	37,240.
11A	48"	Oak	37,240.
11A	48"	Walnut	38,220.
11A	48"	Cherry	38,220.
11A	48"	Polished Woods (above)	39,200.
11A	48"	Polished White	39,200.
11A	48"	Yew	39,200.
8A	52"	Polished Ebony	42,200.
8A	52"	Mahogany	40,680.
8A	52"	Oak	40,680.
8A	52"	Walnut	42,200.
8A	52"	Cherry	42,200.
8A	52"	Polished Woods (above)	43,540.
8A	52"	Polished White	43,540.
8A	52"	Yew	43,540.
8A	52"	*Add for sostenuto*	2,380.
Grands			
K	5' 2"	Polished Ebony	73,360.
K	5' 2"	Mahogany	70,400.
K	5' 2"	Oak	70,400.
K	5' 2"	Walnut	73,360.
K	5' 2"	Cherry	73,360.
K	5' 2"	Polished Woods (above)	75,760.
K	5' 2"	Polished White	75,760.
K	5' 2"	Yew	75,760.
K	5' 2"	Chippendale Mahogany	76,880.
K	5' 2"	Chippendale Oak	76,880.
K	5' 2"	Chippendale Cherry	79,820.
K	5' 2"	Chippendale Walnut	79,820.
K	5' 2"	Chippendale Polished Woods (above)	81,780.
M	5' 11"	Polished Ebony	80,860.
M	5' 11"	Mahogany	77,930.
M	5' 11"	Oak	77,930.
M	5' 11"	Walnut	80,860.

Model	Size	Style and Finish	Price*
M	5' 11"	Cherry	80,860.
M	5' 11"	Polished Woods (above)	84,280.
M	5' 11"	Polished White	84,280.
M	5' 11"	Yew	84,280.
M	5' 11"	Chippendale Mahogany	85,480.
M	5' 11"	Chippendale Oak	85,480.
M	5' 11"	Chippendale Cherry	88,640.
M	5' 11"	Chippendale Walnut	88,640.
M	5' 11"	Chippendale Polished Woods (above)	90,080.
M	5' 11"	Classic Polished Ebony	90,080.
M	5' 11"	Classic Mahogany	87,120.
M	5' 11"	Classic Oak	87,120.
M	5' 11"	Classic Walnut	90,080.
M	5' 11"	Classic Cherry	90,080.
M	5' 11"	Classic Polished Woods (above)	93,680.
M	5' 11"	Classic Polished White	93,680.
M	5' 11"	Classic Yew	93,500.
189-A	6' 2"	Polished Ebony	65,780.
189-A	6' 2"	Mahogany	63,840.
189-A	6' 2"	Oak	63,840.
189-A	6' 2"	Walnut	65,780.
189-A	6' 2"	Cherry	65,780.
189-A	6' 2"	Polished White	68,240.
B	6' 10"	Polished Ebony	90,600.
B	6' 10"	Mahogany	89,200.
B	6' 10"	Oak	89,200.
B	6' 10"	Walnut	90,600.
B	6' 10"	Cherry	90,600.
B	6' 10"	Polished White	93,500.
B	6' 10"	Yew	93,500.
C	7' 6"	Polished Ebony	108,940.
EN	9' 2"	Polished Ebony	135,240.

*For explanation of terms and prices, please see pages 19–24.

Model	Size	Style and Finish	Price*

Becker, J.

Verticals

BV-101	47"	Polished Ebony	2,498.
BV-101	47"	Mahogany	2,558.
BV-101	47"	Polished Mahogany	2,558.
BV-101	47"	Walnut	2,558.
BV-101	47"	Polished Walnut	2,558.
BV-101	47"	Polished Oak	2,598.
BV-101	47"	White	2,598.
BV-201	47"	Polished Ebony	2,698.
BV-201	47"	Mahogany	2,698.
BV-201	47"	Polished Mahogany	2,698.
BV-202	47"	Walnut	2,698.
BV-202	47"	Polished Walnut	2,698.
BV-301	47"	Polished Ebony	2,398.
BV-301	47"	Polished Mahogany	2,498.
BV-301	47"	Polished Walnut	2,498.
BV-301	47"	Polished Birchwood	2,538.

Grands

BG-501	5' 2"	Polished Ebony	7,190.
BG-501	5' 2"	White	7,390.

Betting, Th.

Verticals

M-113CH	44"	Queen Anne Polished Ebony	5,650.
M-113CH	44"	Queen Anne Polished Mahogany	5,650.
M-113CH	44"	Queen Anne Polished Walnut	5,650.
M-113D	44"	Polished Ebony	5,450.
M-113D	44"	Polished Mahogany	5,450.
M-113D	44"	Polished Walnut	5,450.
M-118A	47"	Polished Ebony	5,650.
M-118A	47"	Polished Mahogany	5,650.
M-118A	47"	Polished Walnut	5,650.
M-118A	47"	Oak	5,590.
M-118A	47"	Polished Cherry	5,650.
M-118CH	47"	Chippendale Polished Ebony	5,850.

Model	Size	Style and Finish	Price*
M-118CH	47"	Chippendale Polished Mahogany	5,850.
M-118CH	47"	Chippendale Polished Walnut	5,850.
M-118CH	47"	Chippendale Polished White	6,250.
M-128E	51"	Polished Ebony	6,490.
M-128E	51"	Polished Mahogany	6,490.
M-128E	51"	Polished Walnut	6,490.
Grands			
M-178	5' 8"	Polished Ebony	17,990.

Blüthner

Grands

11	5'	Polished Ebony	40,860.
11	5'	Open-Pore Walnut	39,380.
11	5'	Polished Walnut	42,460.
11	5'	Pyramid Mahogany	52,640.
11	5'	Polished Mahogany	42,460.
10	5' 5"	Polished Ebony	45,860.
10	5' 5"	Open-Pore Walnut	44,180.
10	5' 5"	Polished Walnut	47,860.
10	5' 5"	Pyramid Mahogany	59,950.
10	5' 5"	Polished Mahogany	47,860.
6	6' 2"	Polished Ebony	51,520.
6	6' 2"	Open-Pore Walnut	49,458.
6	6' 2"	Polished Walnut	53,580.
6	6' 2"	Polished Mahogany	53,580.
6	6' 2"	Polished Pyramid Mahogany	66,230.
4	6' 10"	Polished Ebony	59,960.
4	6' 10"	Walnut	57,620.
4	6' 10"	Polished Walnut	61,000.
4	6' 10"	Pyramid Mahogany	74,730.
4	6' 10"	Polished Mahogany	60,268.
2	7' 6"	Polished Ebony	65,870.
1	9'	Polished Ebony	77,960.

*For explanation of terms and prices, please see pages 19–24.

Model	Size	Style and Finish	Price*

Bösendorfer

Verticals

Model	Size	Style and Finish	Price*
130	52"	Polished Ebony	36,980.
130	52"	Walnut	39,980.
130	52"	Open-Pore Walnut	39,980.
130	52"	Polished Walnut	39,980.
130	52"	Mahogany	39,980.
130	52"	Open-Pore Mahogany	39,980.
130	52"	Polished Mahogany	39,980.
130	52"	Polished White	39,980.
130	52"	Polished Pommele	39,980.
130	52"	Rosewood	42,580.

Grands

Model	Size	Style and Finish	Price*
170	5' 8"	Polished Ebony	71,980.
170	5' 8"	Walnut	75,980.
170	5' 8"	Open-Pore Walnut	75,980.
170	5' 8"	Polished Walnut	75,980.
170	5' 8"	Mahogany	75,980.
170	5' 8"	Open-Pore Mahogany	75,980.
170	5' 8"	Polished Mahogany	75,980.
170	5' 8"	Polished White	75,980.
170	5' 8"	Polished Pommele	75,980.
170	5' 8"	Rosewood	80,780.
170	5' 8"	Chippendale Mahogany	80,780.
170	5' 8"	Pyramid Mahogany	80,780.
200	6' 7"	Polished Ebony	83,980.
200	6' 7"	Walnut	91,180.
200	6' 7"	Open-Pore Walnut	91,180.
200	6' 7"	Polished Walnut	91,180.
200	6' 7"	Mahogany	91,180.
200	6' 7"	Open-Pore Mahogany	91,180.
200	6' 7"	Polished Mahogany	91,180.
200	6' 7"	Polished White	91,180.
200	6' 7"	Polished Pommele	91,180.
200	6' 7"	Rosewood	95,580.
200	6' 7"	Chippendale Mahogany	95,580.

Model	Size	Style and Finish	Price*
200	6' 7"	Pyramid Mahogany	95,580.
200	6' 7"	Johann Strauss Polished Ebony	88,980.
200	6' 7"	Senator (various finishes)	97,380.
213	7'	Polished Ebony	95,980.
213	7'	Walnut	105,180.
213	7'	Open-Pore Walnut	105,180.
213	7'	Polished Walnut	105,180.
213	7'	Mahogany	105,180.
213	7'	Open-Pore Mahogany	105,180.
213	7'	Polished Mahogany	105,180.
213	7'	Polished White	105,180.
213	7'	Polished Pommele	105,180.
213	7'	Rosewood	109,980.
213	7'	Chippendale Mahogany	109,980.
213	7'	Pyramid Mahogany	109,980.
213	7'	Johann Strauss Polished Ebony	100,980.
213	7'	Senator (various finishes)	111,780.
225	7' 4"	Polished Ebony	103,980.
225	7' 4"	Walnut	112,780.
225	7' 4"	Open-Pore Walnut	112,780.
225	7' 4"	Polished Walnut	112,780.
225	7' 4"	Mahogany	112,780.
225	7' 4"	Open-Pore Mahogany	112,780.
225	7' 4"	Polished Mahogany	112,780.
225	7' 4"	Polished White	112,780.
225	7' 4"	Polished Pommele	112,780.
225	7' 4"	Rosewood	117,580.
225	7' 4"	Chippendale Mahogany	117,580.
225	7' 4"	Pyramid Mahogany	117,580.
225	7' 4"	Johann Strauss Polished Ebony	108,980.
225	7' 4"	Senator (various finishes)	119,380.
275	9'	Polished Ebony	131,980.
290	9' 6"	Polished Ebony	159,980.

*For explanation of terms and prices, please see pages 19–24.

Model	Size	Style and Finish	Price*
Boston			
Verticals			
UP-109C	43"	Continental Polished Ebony	6,190.
UP-109C	43"	Continental Polished White	6,590.
UP-118C	45"	Continental Polished Ebony	7,100.
UP-118C	45"	Continental Polished White	7,530.
UP-118C	45"	Continental Polished Walnut	7,740.
UP-118E	46"	Polished Ebony	7,530.
UP-118E	46"	Walnut	8,390.
UP-118E	46"	Polished Walnut	8,590.
UP-118E	46"	Polished White	8,390.
UP-118E	46"	Polished Mahogany	8,590.
UP-118S	46"	Honey Oak	5,390.
UP-118S	46"	Black Oak	5,390.
UP-125E	49"	Polished Ebony	8,500.
UP-125E	49"	Polished Mahogany	9,790.
UP-132E	52"	Polished Ebony	10,300.
Grands			
GP-156	5' 1"	Ebony	13,780.
GP-156	5' 1"	Polished Ebony	13,980.
GP-163	5' 4"	Ebony	16,780.
GP-163	5' 4"	Polished Ebony	17,180.
GP-163	5' 4"	Oak	17,580.
GP-163	5' 4"	Mahogany	18,280.
GP-163	5' 4"	Polished Mahogany	18,720.
GP-163	5' 4"	Walnut	18,500.
GP-163	5' 4"	Polished Walnut	18,940.
GP-163	5' 4"	Polished White	17,640.
GP-163	5' 4"	Polished Ivory	17,640.
GP-178	5' 10"	Ebony	19,360.
GP-178	5' 10"	Polished Ebony	19,780.
GP-178	5' 10"	Oak	19,980.
GP-178	5' 10"	Mahogany	20,660.
GP-178	5' 10"	Polished Mahogany	21,080.
GP-178	5' 10"	Walnut	20,880.
GP-178	5' 10"	Polished Walnut	21,520.

Model	Size	Style and Finish	Price*
GP-178	5' 10"	Polished White	20,220.
GP-178	5' 10"	Polished Ivory	20,220.
GP-193	6' 4"	Ebony	24,540.
GP-193	6' 4"	Polished Ebony	25,180.
GP-193	6' 4"	Walnut	27,340.
GP-193	6' 4"	Polished Mahogany	27,540.
GP-193	6' 4"	Polished White	26,480.
GP-218	7' 2"	Ebony	31,180.
GP-218	7' 2"	Polished Ebony	31,980.

Brentwood

Verticals

MP005	42"	Continental Polished Ebony	2,498.
MP005	42"	Continental Polished Mahogany	2,498.
MP005	42"	Continental Polished Dark Walnut	2,498.
MP005	42"	Continental Polished White	2,698.
MP012	46"	Polished Ebony	2,898.
MP012	46"	Polished Mahogany	2,898.
MP012	46"	Polished Dark Walnut	2,898.
MP130	52"	Polished Mahogany	3,590.

Charles R. Walter — see "Walter, Charles R."

Chickering

Grands

410	4' 10"	Ebony	12,180.
410	4' 10"	Polished Ebony	12,700.
410	4' 10"	Mahogany	12,900.
410	4' 10"	Polished Mahogany	13,450.
410	4' 10"	Queen Anne Cherry	13,760.
410	4' 10"	Queen Anne Polished Cherry	14,240.
507	5' 7"	Ebony	14,260.
507	5' 7"	Polished Ebony	14,820.
507	5' 7"	Mahogany	15,160.
507	5' 7"	Polished Mahogany	15,800.

*For explanation of terms and prices, please see pages 19–24.

Model	Size	Style and Finish	Price*

Dobbert, Fritz

Verticals

Model	Size	Style and Finish	Price*
108-04	42-1/2"	Continental Polished Mahogany	5,180.
108-07	42-1/2"	Continental Polished Imbuia	5,180.
108-11	42-1/2"	Continental Polished Ebony	5,180.
108-17	42-1/2"	Continental Imbuia	5,180.
109-04	43"	Polished Mahogany	5,580.
109-07	43"	Polished Imbuia	5,580.
109-11	43"	Polished Ebony	5,580.
109-17	43"	Imbuia	5,380.
113-14	43"	Mahogany	5,780.
116-11	45"	Polished Ebony	5,980.
126-04	50"	Polished Mahogany	7,380.
126-07	50"	Polished Imbuia	7,380.
126-11	50"	Polished Ebony	7,380.
126-17	50"	Imbuia	7,180.
127-04	50"	Polished Mahogany	7,380.
127-07	50"	Polished Imbuia	7,380.
127-11	50"	Polished Ebony	7,380.
127-17	50"	Imbuia	7,180.

Estonia

Grands

Model	Size	Style and Finish	Price*
163	5' 4"	Ebony	13,200.
163	5' 4"	Polished Ebony	13,200.
163	5' 4"	White	13,200.
163	5' 4"	Polished White	13,200.
190	6' 3"	Ebony	16,800.
190	6' 3"	Polished Ebony	16,800.
190	6' 3"	White	16,800.
190	6' 3"	Polished White	16,800.
190	6' 3"	*Above four with Renner action, add*	1,600.
190	6' 3"	Chippendale White	19,400.
190	6' 3"	Chippendale Polished White	19,400.
273	9'	Ebony	29,600.
273	9'	Polished Ebony	29,600.

Model	Size	Style and Finish	Price*

Fandrich

Verticals
Artist	48"	Ebony	14,800.

Fazioli

Grands
F156	5' 2"	Ebony	65,400.
F156	5' 2"	Polished Ebony	66,800.
F156	5' 2"	Walnut	68,400.
F156	5' 2"	Polished Walnut	71,600.
F156	5' 2"	Polished Pyramid Mahogany	73,900.
F156	5' 2"	Cherry	68,400.
F156	5' 2"	Polished Cherry	71,600.
F183	6'	Ebony	72,800.
F183	6'	Polished Ebony	74,400.
F183	6'	Walnut	76,400.
F183	6'	Polished Walnut	79,800.
F183	6'	Polished Pyramid Mahogany	82,700.
F183	6'	Cherry	76,400.
F183	6'	Polished Cherry	79,800
F212	6' 11"	Ebony	81,900.
F212	6' 11"	Polished Ebony	83,900.
F212	6' 11"	Walnut	85,900.
F212	6' 11"	Polished Walnut	89,900.
F212	6' 11"	Polished Pyramid Mahogany	93,000.
F212	6' 11"	Cherry	85,900.
F212	6' 11"	Polished Cherry	89,900.
F228	7' 6"	Ebony	91,900.
F228	7' 6"	Polished Ebony	93,900.
F228	7' 6"	Walnut	95,900.
F228	7' 6"	Polished Walnut	99,900.
F228	7' 6"	Polished Pyramid Mahogany	103,900.
F228	7' 6"	Cherry	95,900.
F228	7' 6"	Polished Cherry	99,900.
F278	9' 2"	Ebony	117,900.
F278	9' 2"	Polished Ebony	119,900.

*For explanation of terms and prices, please see pages 19–24.

Model	Size	Style and Finish	Price*
Fazioli (continued)			
F278	9' 2"	Walnut	123,200.
F278	9' 2"	Polished Walnut	128,700.
F278	9' 2"	Polished Pyramid Mahogany	133,200.
F278	9' 2"	Cherry	123,200.
F278	9' 2"	Polished Cherry	128,700.
F308	10' 2"	Ebony	155,500.
F308	10' 2"	Polished Ebony	157,900.
F308	10' 2"	Walnut	161,500.
F308	10' 2"	Polished Walnut	165,900.
F308	10' 2"	Polished Pyramid Mahogany	171,900.
F308	10' 2"	Cherry	161,500.
F308	10' 2"	Polished Cherry	165,900.

Feurich

Grands

Model	Size	Style and Finish	Price*
F173	5' 8"	Polished Ebony	36,380.
F173	5' 8"	Polished Mahogany	37,180.
F173	5' 8"	Polished Walnut	37,180.
F173	5' 8"	Polished White	37,380.
F208	6' 8"	Polished Ebony	42,780.
F208	6' 8"	Polished Mahogany	43,580.
F208	6' 8"	Polished Walnut	43,580.
F208	6' 8"	Polished White	43,780.

Förster, August

Verticals

Model	Size	Style and Finish	Price*
116C	46"	Chippendale Polished Ebony	17,220.
116C	46"	Chippendale Polished Walnut	17,220.
116E	46"	Polished Ebony	17,220.
116	46"	Polished White	18,092.
125G	50"	Polished Ebony	20,710.
125	50"	Polished White	21,582.
Grands			
170	5' 7"	Polished Ebony	35,970.

Model	Size	Style and Finish	Price*
170	5' 7"	Polished Walnut	35,970.
170	5' 7"	Polished Mahogany	35,970.
170	5' 7"	Chippendale	39,450.
170	5' 7"	Antique	42,510.
170	5' 7"	Polished White	37,930.
170	5' 7"	Rococo	68,670.
190	6' 4"	Polished Ebony	40,330.
190	6' 4"	Polished Walnut	40,330.
190	6' 4"	Polished Mahogany	40,330.
190	6' 4"	Chippendale	43,810.
190	6' 4"	Antique	46,870.
190	6' 4"	Polished White	42,290.
215	7' 4"	Polished Ebony	50,140.
275	9' 2"	Polished Ebony	71,940.

Fritz Dobbert — See "Dobbert, Fritz"

Grotrian

Grands

Model	Size	Style and Finish	Price*
165	5' 5"	Ebony	40,000.
165	5' 5"	Polished Ebony	45,000.
165	5' 5"	Polished Walnut	49,000.
165	5' 5"	Polished Mahogany	49,000.
192	6' 3"	Ebony	46,000.
192	6' 3"	Polished Ebony	51,000.
192	6' 3"	Polished Walnut	55,000.
192	6' 3"	Polished Mahogany	55,000.
225	7' 5"	Ebony	58,000.
225	7' 5"	Polished Ebony	63,000.
225	7' 5"	Polished Walnut	67,000.
225	7' 5"	Polished Mahogany	67,000.
277	9' 2"	Polished Ebony	80,000.

*For explanation of terms and prices, please see pages 19–24.

Model	Size	Style and Finish	Price*

Hastings

Verticals

Model	Size	Style and Finish	Price*
MY108-B	43"	Continental Polished Ebony	2,810.
MY108-B	43"	Continental Polished White	2,810.
MY108-B	43"	Continental Polished Walnut	2,810.
MY108-B	43"	Continental Polished Mahogany	2,810.
MY108-D	43"	Polished Ebony	2,870.
MY108-D	43"	Polished White	2,870.
MY108-D	43"	Polished Walnut	2,870.
MY108-D	43"	Polished Mahogany	2,870.
MY108-DA3	43"	Chippendale Polished Ebony	3,060.
MY108-DA3	43"	Chippendale Polished White	3,060.
MY108-DA3	43"	Chippendale Polished Walnut	3,060.
MY108-DA3	43"	Chippendale Polished Mahogany	3,060.
MY108-E	43"	Continental Polished Ebony	2,760.
MY108-E	43"	Continental Polished White	2,760.
MY108-E	43"	Continental Polished Walnut	2,760.
MY108-E	43"	Continental Polished Mahogany	2,760.
MY115-B	45"	Continental Polished Ebony	2,810.
MY115-B	45"	Continental Polished White	2,810.
MY115-B	45"	Continental Polished Walnut	2,810.
MY115-B	45"	Continental Polished Mahogany	2,810.
MY118-A3	46"	Chippendale Polished Ebony	3,330.
MY118-A3	46"	Chippendale Polished White	3,330.
MY118-A3	46"	Chippendale Polished Walnut	3,330.
MY118-A3	46"	Chippendale Polished Mahogany	3,330.
MY118-A3M	46"	Chippendale Polished Ebony	3,530.
MY118-A3M	46"	Chippendale Polished White	3,530.
MY118-F	46"	Polished Ebony	3,100.
MY118-F	46"	Polished White	3,100.
MY118-F	46"	Polished Walnut	3,100.
MY118-F	46"	Polished Mahogany	3,100.
MY118-F2	46"	Polished Ebony	3,350.
MY118-F2	46"	Polished White	3,350.
MY118-F2	46"	Polished Walnut	3,350.
MY118-F2	46"	Polished Mahogany	3,350.

Model	Size	Style and Finish	Price*
MY130-A1	51"	Polished Ebony	3,690.
MY130-A1	51"	Polished White	3,690.
MY130-A1	51"	Polished Walnut	3,690.
MY130-A1	51"	Polished Mahogany	3,690.

Hyundai

Verticals

Model	Size	Style and Finish	Price*
U-810	41"	Continental Ebony	3,598.
U-810	41"	Continental Polished Ebony	3,798.
U-810	41"	Continental Walnut	3,978.
U-810	41"	Continental Polished Walnut	3,978.
U-810	41"	Continental Polished Mahogany	3,978.
U-810	41"	Continental Polished Ivory	3,918.
U-810	41"	Continental Polished White	3,918.
U-810	41"	Continental Polished Dark Oak	3,978.
U-810	41"	Continental Polished Rosewood	3,978.
U-810	41"	Continental Brown Oak	3,978.
U-821	42"	Continental Polished Ebony	3,998.
U-821	42"	Continental Polished Walnut	4,258.
U-821	42"	Continental Polished Mahogany	4,258.
U-821	42"	Continental Polished Ivory	4,178.
U-821	42"	Continental Polished White	4,178.
U-824F	43"	French Walnut	4,798.
U-824F	43"	French Oak	4,798.
U-824F	43"	French Cherry	4,798.
U-824M	43"	Mediterranean Brown Oak	4,798.
U-824T	43"	Cherry	4,798.
U-822	45"	Continental Polished Ebony	4,398.
U-822	45"	Continental Polished Walnut	4,598.
U-822	45"	Continental Polished Mahogany	4,598.
U-822	45"	Continental Polished Ivory	4,520.
U-822	45"	Continental Polished White	4,520.
U-822	45"	Continental Brown Oak	4,598.
U-822	45"	Continental Polished Brown Oak	4,598.
U-852	46"	Ebony	4,958.
U-852	46"	Polished Ebony	5,058.

*For explanation of terms and prices, please see pages 19–24.

Model	Size	Style and Finish	Price*
Hyundai (continued)			
U-852	46"	Brown Oak	5,118.
U-852	46"	Walnut	5,118.
U-842	46"	Chippendale Polished Mahogany	5,398.
U-832	48"	Ebony	4,998.
U-832	48"	Polished Ebony	5,100.
U-832	48"	Walnut	5,198.
U-832	48"	Polished Walnut	5,198.
U-832	48"	Oak	5,198.
U-832	48"	Polished Dark Oak	5,198.
U-832	48"	Polished Mahogany	5,198.
U-837	52"	Ebony	5,398.
U-837	52"	Polished Ebony	5,498.
U-837	52"	Walnut	5,598.
U-837	52"	Polished Walnut	5,598.
U-837	52"	Polished Mahogany	5,598.
Grands			
G-50A	4' 7"	Ebony	9,100.
G-50A	4' 7"	Polished Ebony	9,398.
G-50A	4' 7"	Walnut	9,798.
G-50A	4' 7"	Polished Walnut	9,798.
G-50A	4' 7"	Polished Mahogany	9,798.
G-50A	4' 7"	Brown Oak	9,798.
G-50A	4' 7"	Polished Brown Oak	9,798.
G-50A	4' 7"	Polished Natural Oak	9,798.
G-50A	4' 7"	Cherry	9,798.
G-50A	4' 7"	Polished Ivory	9,598.
G-50A	4' 7"	Polished White	9,598.
G-50A	4' 7"	Polished Rosewood	9,900.
G-50AF	4' 7"	Queen Anne Polished Ebony	11,198.
G-50AF	4' 7"	Queen Anne Walnut	11,198.
G-50AF	4' 7"	Queen Anne Polished Walnut	11,198.
G-50AF	4' 7"	Queen Anne Brown Oak	11,198.
G-50AF	4' 7"	Queen Anne Polished Brown Oak	11,198.
G-50AF	4' 7"	Queen Anne Polished Mahogany	11,198.
G-50AF	4' 7"	Queen Anne Cherry	11,198.

Model	Size	Style and Finish	Price*
G-50AF	4' 7"	Queen Anne Polished Ivory	11,198.
G-50AF	4' 7"	Queen Anne Polished White	11,198.
G-80A	5' 1"	Ebony	10,598.
G-80A	5' 1"	Polished Ebony	10,998.
G-80A	5' 1"	Walnut	11,398.
G-80A	5' 1"	Polished Walnut	11,398.
G-80A	5' 1"	Oak	11,398.
G-80A	5' 1"	Polished Oak	11,398.
G-80A	5' 1"	Polished Mahogany	11,398.
G-80A	5' 1"	Cherry	11,398.
G-80A	5' 1"	Polished Ivory	11,198.
G-80A	5' 1"	Polished White	11,198.
G-80B	5' 1"	Chippendale Polished Mahogany	13,598.
G-80B	5' 1"	Chippendale Polished White	13,598.
G-81	5' 9"	Chippendale Polished Mahogany	14,998.
G-82	5' 9"	Ebony	11,998.
G-82	5' 9"	Polished Ebony	12,398.
G-82	5' 9"	Walnut	12,798.
G-82	5' 9"	Polished Walnut	12,798.
G-82	5' 9"	Oak	12,798.
G-82	5' 9"	Polished Oak	12,798.
G-82	5' 9"	Polished Mahogany	12,798.
G-82	5' 9"	Cherry	12,798.
G-82	5' 9"	Polished Rosewood	12,900.
G-82	5' 9"	Polished Ivory	12,598.
G-82	5' 9"	Polished White	12,598.
G-84	6' 1"	Ebony	12,998.
G-84	6' 1"	Polished Ebony	13,198.
G-84	6' 1"	Walnut	13,598.
G-84	6' 1"	Polished Walnut	13,598.
G-84	6' 1"	Oak	13,598.
G-84	6' 1"	Polished Oak	13,598.
G-84	6' 1"	Polished Mahogany	13,598.
G-84	6' 1"	Polished Ivory	13,398.
G-84	6' 1"	Polished White	13,398.
G-85	6' 10"	Ebony	16,998.
G-85	6' 10"	Polished Ebony	16,998.

*For explanation of terms and prices, please see pages 19–24.

Model	Size	Style and Finish	Price*

Kawai

Verticals

Model	Size	Style and Finish	Price*
CX-5	41"	Continental Polished Ebony	5,030.
CX-5	41"	Continental Polished Mahogany	5,150.
CX-5	41"	Continental Polished Snow White	5,070.
CX-5	41"	Continental Polished Ivory	5,070.
502-S	43"	Ebony	4,090.
502-S	43"	Oak	4,090.
503-F	43"	French Provincial Cherry	4,410.
503-M	43"	Mediterranean Oak	4,290.
503-M	43"	Mediterranean Pecan	4,290.
503-Q	43"	Queen Anne Mahogany	4,410.
503-T	43"	Mahogany	4,290.
AT-503-M	43"	Mediterranean Oak with AnyTime	5,750.
AT-503-F	43"	French Provincial Cherry with AnyTime	5,870.
603-CF	44"	Country French Oak	5,210.
603-F	44"	French Provincial Cherry	5,210.
603-M	44"	Mediterranean Pecan	5,090.
603-T	44"	Mahogany	5,170.
CE-11	44"	Continental Polished Ebony	6,770.
CE-11	44"	Continental Polished Sapeli Mahogany	7,370.
902-F	46"	French Provincial Cherry	6,290.
902-M	46"	Mediterranean Oak	6,070.
902-T	46"	Mahogany	6,290.
UST-7	46"	Ebony	5,970.
UST-7	46"	Oak	6,210.
UST-7	46"	Walnut	6,250.
UST-8C	46"	Ebony	5,050.
UST-8C	46"	Oak	5,050.
UST-8C	46"	Walnut	5,050.
CX-21	48"	Polished Ebony	5,470.
CX-21	48"	Polished Snow White	5,470.
AT-120	48"	Polished Ebony with AnyTime	6,490.
NS-20A	49"	Polished Ebony	7,210.
NS-20A	49"	Oak	7,630.
NS-20A	49"	Walnut	7,850.

Model	Size	Style and Finish	Price*
NS-20A	49"	Polished Walnut	8,330.
NS-20A	49"	Polished Sapeli Mahogany	8,190.
AT-170	49"	Polished Ebony with AnyTime	8,590.
US-6X	52"	Polished Ebony	9,590.
US-6X	52"	Polished Walnut	10,850.
US-8X	52"	Polished Ebony	11,750.
Grands			
GM-1	4' 9"	Ebony	11,690.
GM-1	4' 9"	Polished Ebony	11,790.
GM-1	4' 9"	Polished Snow White	12,790.
GE-1	5' 1"	Ebony	12,890.
GE-1	5' 1"	Polished Ebony	13,050.
GE-1	5' 1"	Walnut	14,590.
GE-1	5' 1"	Polished White	14,390.
GE-1	5' 1"	Polished Ivory	14,590.
RX-1	5' 5"	Ebony	16,690.
RX-1	5' 5"	Polished Ebony	16,990.
RX-1	5' 5"	Walnut	18,990.
RX-1	5' 5"	Polished Walnut	19,790.
RX-1	5' 5"	Polished Sapeli Mahogany	19,590.
RX-1	5' 5'	Polished White	18,790.
GE-3	5' 9"	Polished Ebony	17,390.
GE-3	5' 9"	Polished Snow White	18,790.
RX-2	5' 10"	Ebony	18,790.
RX-2	5' 10"	Polished Ebony	19,190.
RX-2	5' 10"	Walnut	20,790.
RX-2	5' 10"	Polished Walnut	21,590.
RX-2	5' 10"	Oak	19,790.
RX-2	5' 10"	Polished Sapeli Mahogany	21,190.
RX-2	5' 10"	Polished Mahogany	21,790.
RX-2	5' 10"	Polished White	20,390.
RX-2	5' 10"	Polished Rosewood	25,090.
RX-2F	5' 10"	French Provincial Polished Mahogany	25,090.
RX-3	6' 1"	Ebony	25,290.
RX-3	6' 1"	Polished Ebony	26,190.
RX-A	6' 5"	Polished Ebony	51,990.
RX-5	6' 6"	Ebony	27,990.

*For explanation of terms and prices, please see pages 19–24.

Model	Size	Style and Finish	Price*

Kawai (continued)

Model	Size	Style and Finish	Price
RX-5	6' 6"	Polished Ebony	28,390.
RX-6	7'	Ebony	30,990.
RX-6	7'	Polished Ebony	31,390.
GS-100	9' 1"	Ebony	66,790.
GS-100	9' 1"	Polished Ebony	68,790.
EX	9' 1"	Polished Ebony	98,990.

Knabe

These are the pianos formerly known as "PianoDisc". Models and prices should be considered tentative. Models listed include a PianoDisc playback system installed in the piano.

Verticals

Model	Size	Style and Finish	Price
KN420	42"	Continental Polished Ebony	7,990.
KN420	42"	Continental Polished Walnut	8,390.
KN420	42"	Continental Polished Mahogany	8,390.
KN420	42"	Continental Polished Ivory	7,990.
KN420	42"	Continental Polished White	7,990.
KNF43	43"	Queen Anne Oak	9,390.
KNF43	43"	Queen Anne Cherry	9,390.
KN480	48"	Ebony	9,590.
KN480	48"	Polished Ebony	9,590.
KN480	48"	Walnut	9,990.
KN480	48"	Walnut Lilly	10,190.
KN480	48"	Polished Mahogany	9,990.
KN480	48"	Polished Ivory	9,590.
KN480	48"	Polished White	9,590.

Grands

Model	Size	Style and Finish	Price
KN500	4' 11"	Ebony	14,790.
KN500	4' 11"	Polished Ebony	14,790.
KN500	4' 11"	Walnut	15,590.
KN500	4' 11"	Polished Mahogany	15,590.
KN500	4' 11"	Polished Ivory	14,790.
KN500	4' 11"	Polished White	14,790.
KN500QA	4' 11"	Queen Anne Mahogany	17,990.
KN500QA	4' 11"	Queen Anne Polished Mahogany	17,990.

Model	Size	Style and Finish	Price*
KN520	5' 2"	Ebony	15,990.
KN520	5' 2"	Polished Ebony	15,990.
KN520	5' 2"	Walnut	16,890.
KN520	5' 2"	Polished Mahogany	16,890.
KN520	5' 2"	Polished Ivory	15,990.
KN520	5' 2"	Polished White	15,990.
KN520QA	5' 2"	Queen Anne Cherry	18,790.
KN520QA	5' 2"	Queen Anne Mahogany	18,790.
KN590	5' 9"	Polished Ebony	16,990.
KN590	5' 9"	Polished Walnut	17,590.
KN590	5' 9"	Polished Mahogany	17,590.
KN590	5' 9"	Polished Ivory	16,990.
KN590	5' 9"	Polished White	16,990.
KN590	5' 9"	Empire Mahogany	19,990.
KN610	6' 1"	Ebony	17,990.
KN610	6' 1"	Polished Ebony	17,990.
KN610	6' 1"	Walnut	18,590.
KN610	6' 1"	Polished Mahogany	18,590.
KN610	6' 1"	Polished Ivory	17,990.
KN610	6' 1"	Polished White	17,990.
KN700	6' 10"	Polished Ebony	19,590.

Kohler & Campbell

Verticals

Model	Size	Style and Finish	Price*
SKV-108S	42"	Continental Ebony	3,790.
SKV-108S	42"	Continental Polished Ebony	3,790.
SKV-108S	42"	Continental Walnut	3,890.
SKV-108S	42"	Continental Polished Walnut	3,890.
SKV-108S	42"	Continental Polished Mahogany	3,890.
SKV-108S	42"	Continental Oak	3,890.
SKV-108S	42"	Continental Polished Oak	3,890.
SKV-108S	42"	Continental Polished Ivory	3,790.
SKV-108S	42"	Continental Polished White	3,790.
SKV-430FS	43"	French Provincial Cherry	3,990.
SKV-430FS	43"	French Provincial Oak	3,990.
SKV-430MS	43"	Mediterranean Oak	3,790.

*For explanation of terms and prices, please see pages 19–24.

Model	Size	Style and Finish	Price*

Kohler & Campbell (continued)

Model	Size	Style and Finish	Price*
SKV-430TS	43"	Cherry	3,890.
SKV-465S	46-1/2"	Ebony	4,490.
SKV-465S	46-1/2"	Polished Ebony	4,490.
SKV-465S	46-1/2"	Walnut	4,490.
SKV-465S	46-1/2"	Polished Walnut	4,490.
SKV-465S	46-1/2"	Mahogany	4,490.
SKV-465S	46-1/2"	Polished Mahogany	4,490.
SKV-465S	46-1/2"	Oak	4,490.
SKV-465S	46-1/2"	Polished Oak	4,490.
SKV-470TS	46-1/2"	Cherry	4,490.
SKV-470FS	46-1/2"	French Provincial Oak	4,590.
SKV-470FS	46-1/2"	French Provincial Cherry	4,590.
SKV-470MS	46-1/2"	Mediterranean Oak	4,390.
SKV-48S	48"	Ebony	5,160.
SKV-48S	48"	Polished Ebony	5,160.
SKV-48S	48"	Walnut	5,260.
SKV-48S	48"	Polished Walnut	5,260.
SKV-48S	48"	Oak	5,260.
SKV-48S	48"	Polished Oak	5,260.
SKV-48S	48"	Polished Mahogany	5,260.
SKV-48S	48"	Polished Ivory	5,260.
SKV-48S	48"	Polished White	5,260.
SKV-52S	52"	Ebony	5,660.
SKV-52S	52"	Polished Ebony	5,660.
SKV-52S	52"	Walnut	5,760.
SKV-52S	52"	Polished Walnut	5,760.
SKV-52S	52"	Polished Mahogany	5,760.
SKV-52S	52"	Polished White	5,760.

Grands

Model	Size	Style and Finish	Price*
SKG-400S	4' 7"	Ebony	8,590.
SKG-400S	4' 7"	Polished Ebony	8,590.
SKG-400S	4' 7"	Walnut	9,190.
SKG-400S	4' 7"	Polished Walnut	9,190.
SKG-400S	4' 7"	Mahogany	9,190.
SKG-400S	4' 7"	Polished Mahogany	9,190.

Model	Size	Style and Finish	Price*
SKG-400S	4' 7"	Oak	9,190.
SKG-400S	4' 7"	Polished Oak	9,190.
SKG-400S	4' 7"	Cherry	9,190.
SKG-400S	4' 7"	Polished Ivory	8,990.
SKG-400S	4' 7"	Polished White	8,990.
SKG-400CAF	4' 7"	French Provincial Walnut	11,250.
SKG-400CBF	4' 7"	French Provincial Polished Walnut	11,630.
SKG-400CBF	4' 7"	French Provincial Polished Mahogany	11,630.
SKG-500S	5' 1"	Ebony	10,590.
SKG-500S	5' 1"	Polished Ebony	10,590.
SKG-500S	5' 1"	Walnut	10,890.
SKG-500S	5' 1"	Polished Walnut	10,890.
SKG-500S	5' 1'	Mahogany	10,890.
SKG-500S	5' 1"	Polished Mahogany	10,890.
SKG-500S	5' 1"	Oak	10,890.
SKG-500S	5' 1"	Polished Oak	10,890.
SKG-500S	5' 1"	Cherry	10,890.
SKG-500S	5' 1"	Polished Ivory	10,590.
SKG-500S	5' 1"	Polished White	10,590.
SKG-600S	5' 9"	Ebony	11,890.
SKG-600S	5' 9"	Polished Ebony	11,890.
SKG-600S	5' 9"	Walnut	12,190.
SKG-600S	5' 9"	Polished Walnut	12,190.
SKG-600S	5' 9"	Mahogany	12,190.
SKG-600S	5' 9"	Polished Mahogany	12,190.
SKG-600S	5' 9"	Oak	12,190.
SKG-600S	5' 9"	Polished Oak	12,190.
SKG-600S	5' 9"	Cherry	12,190.
SKG-600S	5' 9"	Polished Ivory	11,890.
SKG-600S	5' 9"	White	11,890.
SKG-600S	5' 9"	Polished White	11,890.
SKG-650S	5' 9"	Ebony	13,040.
SKG-650S	6' 1"	Polished Ebony	13,040.
SKG-650S	6' 1"	Walnut	13,340.
SKG-650S	6' 1"	Polished Walnut	13,340.
SKG-650S	6' 1"	Mahogany	13,340.
SKG-650S	6' 1"	Polished Mahogany	13,340.

*For explanation of terms and prices, please see pages 19–24.

Model	Size	Style and Finish	Price*

Kohler & Campbell (continued)

SKG-650S	6' 1"	Oak	13,340.
SKG-650S	6' 1"	Polished Oak	13,340.
SKG-650S	6' 1"	Cherry	13,340.
SKG-700S	6' 10"	Ebony	18,500.
SKG-700S	6' 10"	Polished Ebony	18,500.
SKG-800S	7'	Ebony	22,590.
SKG-800S	7'	Polished Ebony	22,590.

Kranich & Bach

Verticals

BP50	42"	Continental Polished Ebony	2,590.
BP50	42"	Continental Polished Cherry	2,590.

Maeari

Verticals

MU810	41"	Continental Ebony	3,598.
MU810	41"	Continental Polished Ebony	3,798.
MU810	41"	Continental Polished Walnut	3,978.
MU810	41"	Continental Polished Mahogany	3,978.
MU810	41"	Continental Oak	3,620.
MU810	41"	Continental Polished Oak	3,620.
MU810	41"	Continental Brown Oak	3,978.
MU810	41"	Continental Polished Ivory	3,918.
MU810	41"	Continental Polished White	3,918.
MU821	42"	Continental Polished Ebony	3,998.
MU824F	43"	French Brown Oak	4,798.
MU824F	43"	French Cherry	4,798.
MU824M	43"	Mediterranean Brown Oak	4,798.
MU824T	43"	Brown Oak	4,798.
MU852	46"	Polished Ebony	5,058.
MU852	46"	Walnut	5,118.
MU852	46"	Brown Oak	5,118.
MU842	46"	Chippendale Polished Walnut	5,398.
MU842	46"	Chippendale Polished Mahogany	5,398.

Model	Size	Style and Finish	Price*
MU832	48"	Polished Ebony	5,100.
MU832	48"	Polished Walnut	5,198.
MU832	48"	Polished Mahogany	5,198.
MU837	52"	Polished Ebony	5,498.
MU837	52"	Polished Mahogany	5,498.
Grands			
G-450A	4' 7"	Ebony	9,100.
G-450A	4' 7"	Polished Ebony	9,398.
G-450A	4' 7"	Walnut	9,798.
G-450A	4' 7"	Polished Walnut	9,798.
G-450A	4' 7"	Polished Mahogany	9,798.
G-450A	4' 7"	Cherry	9,798.
G-450A	4' 7"	Polished Oak	9,798.
G-450A	4' 7"	Polished Rosewood	9,900.
G-450A	4' 7"	Polished Ivory	9,598.
G-450A	4' 7"	Polished White	9,598.
G-450AF	4' 7"	Queen Anne Polished Ebony	11,198.
G-450AF	4' 7"	Queen Anne Walnut	11,198.
G-450AF	4' 7"	Queen Anne Polished Walnut	11,198.
G-450AF	4' 7"	Queen Anne Polished Mahogany	11,198.
G-450AF	4' 7"	Queen Anne Cherry	11,198.
G-450AF	4' 7"	Queen Anne Oak	11,198.
G-450AF	4' 7"	Queen Anne Polished Oak	11,198.
G-480A	5' 1"	Ebony	10,598.
G-480A	5' 1"	Polished Ebony	10,998.
G-480A	5' 1"	Walnut	11,398.
G-480A	5' 1"	Polished Walnut	11,398.
G-480A	5' 1"	Polished Mahogany	11,398.
G-480A	5' 1"	Cherry	11,398.
G-480A	5' 1"	Polished Oak	11,398.
G-480A	5' 1"	Polished Ivory	11,198.
G-480A	5' 1"	Polished White	11,198.
G-480B	5' 1"	Chippendale Polished Mahogany	13,598.
G-482	5' 9"	Polished Ebony	12,398.
G-482	5' 9"	Walnut	12,798.
G-482	5' 9"	Polished Walnut	12,798.
G-482	5' 9"	Polished Mahogany	12,798.

*For explanation of terms and prices, please see pages 19–24.

Model	Size	Style and Finish	Price*

Maeari (continued)

Model	Size	Style and Finish	Price*
G-482	5' 9"	Polished Ivory	12,598.
G-482	5' 9"	Polished White	12,598.
G-482	5' 9"	Chippendale Polished Mahogany	14,998.
G-484	6' 1"	Polished Ebony	13,198.
G-484	6' 1"	Polished Mahogany	13,598.
G-484	6' 1"	Polished Ivory	13,398.
G-485	6' 10"	Ebony	16,998.
G-485	6' 10"	Polished Ebony	16,998.

Mason & Hamlin

Model and price information not available at press time.

Verticals

50	50"

Grands

A	5' 8"
BB	7'

Nakamura (formerly Nakamichi)

Verticals

Model	Size	Style and Finish	Price*
N-121	48"	Polished Ebony	5,990.
N-121	48"	Polished Mahogany	6,790.
N-131	52"	Polished Ebony	6,990.
N-131	52"	Polished Mahogany	7,790.

Grands

Model	Size	Style and Finish	Price*
N-157	5' 2"	Polished Ebony	13,990.
N-157	5' 2"	Polished Mahogany	14,990.
N-185	6' 1"	Polished Ebony	15,590.
N-185	6' 1"	Polished Mahogany	16,590.

Pearl River

Verticals

Model	Size	Style and Finish	Price*
UP-108B	43"	Continental Polished Ebony	2,870.
UP-108B	43"	Continental Polished Walnut	2,870.

Model	Size	Style and Finish	Price*
UP-108B	43"	Continental Polished Mahogany	2,870.
UP-108B	43"	Continental Walnut Veneer	3,070.
UP-108B	43"	Continental Polished White	2,870.
UP-108M	43"	Polished Ebony	2,870.
UP-110R	43"	Walnut	3,470.
UP-108M	43"	Polished Walnut	2,870.
UP-108M	43"	Polished Mahogany	2,870.
UP-110R	43"	Cherry	3,470.
UP-108M	43"	Polished White	2,870.
UP-108M2	43"	Chippendale Polished Ebony	2,950.
UP-108M2	43"	Chippendale Polished Walnut	2,950.
UP-114B	45"	Continental Polished Ebony	2,910.
UP-114B	45"	Continental Polished Walnut	2,910.
UP-114B	45"	Continental Polished Mahogany	2,910.
UP-114B	45"	Continental Polished White	2,910.
UP-115M	45"	Polished Ebony	2,970.
UP-115M	45"	Polished Walnut	2,970.
UP-115M	45"	Polished Mahogany	2,970.
UP-115M	45"	Polished White	2,970.
UP-118M	46"	Polished Ebony	3,150.
UP-118M	46"	Polished White	3,150.
UP-118M2	46"	Chippendale Polished Walnut	3,390.
UP-118M2	46"	Chippendale Polished Mahogany	3,390.
UP-121M	48"	Polished Ebony	3,750.
UP-121M	48"	Polished Walnut	3,750.
UP-130M	51"	Polished Ebony	3,670.
UP-130M	51"	Polished Walnut	3,670.
UP-130M1	51"	Chippendale Polished Walnut	3,990.
UP-130M1	51"	Chippendale Polished Mahogany	3,990.

Grands

Model	Size	Style and Finish	Price*
GP-159	5' 2-1/2"	Polished Ebony	8,990.
GP-159	5' 2-1/2"	Polished Mahogany	9,190.
GP-159	5' 2-1/2"	Polished White	9,190.

*For explanation of terms and prices, please see pages 19–24.

Model	Size	Style and Finish	Price*

Petrof

Verticals

Model	Size	Style and Finish	Price*
100-B	42"	Barok Polished Walnut	6,100.
100-B	42"	Barok Polished Flame Mahogany	6,100.
100-S	42"	Continental Polished Ebony	4,980.
100-S	42"	Continental Polished Walnut	4,980.
100-S	42"	Continental Polished Flame Mahogany	4,980.
105-I	42"	Antique Polished Ebony	5,580.
105-I	42"	Antique Polished Walnut	5,580.
105-I	42"	Antique Polished Flame Mahogany	5,580.
115-I	45"	Demi-Chippendale Polished Ebony	5,700.
115-I	45"	Demi-Chippendale Polished Walnut	5,700.
115-I	45"	Demi-Chippendale Pol. Flam. Mahogany	5,700.
115-I	45"	Rococo White with Gold Trim	6,500.
115-IC	45"	Chippendale Polished Ebony	5,980.
115-IC	45"	Chippendale Polished Walnut	5,980.
115-IC	45"	Chippendale Polished Flame Mahogany	5,980.
115-II	45"	Continental Polished Ebony	5,180.
115-II	45"	Continental Polished Walnut	5,180.
115-II	45"	Continental Polished Flame Mahogany	5,180.
115-II	45"	Continental Polished Oak	5,180.
115-IID	45"	Polished Ebony	5,700.
115-IID	45"	Polished Walnut	5,700.
115-IID	45"	Polished Flame Mahogany	5,700.
115-VI	45"	Polished Ebony	5,500.
115-VI	45"	Polished Walnut	5,500.
115-VI	45"	Polished Flame Mahogany	5,500.
125-II	50"	Polished Ebony	6,380.
125-II	50"	Polished Walnut	6,380.
125-II	50"	Polished Flame Mahogany	6,380.
126	50"	Polished Ebony with Walnut trim	6,980.
131	52"	Polished Ebony	9,380.
131	52"	Polished Walnut	9,380.
131	52"	Polished Flame Mahogany	9,380.

Grands

Model	Size	Style and Finish	Price*
V	5' 3"	Polished Ebony	15,980.

Model	Size	Style and Finish	Price*
V	5' 3"	Polished Walnut	15,980.
V	5' 3"	Polished Flame Mahogany	15,980.
V	5' 3"	Polished White	16,780.
IV	5' 8"	Polished Ebony	17,180.
IV	5' 8"	Polished Walnut	17,180.
IV	5' 8"	Polished Flame Mahogany	17,180.
IV	5' 8"	Polished White	17,980.
IV C	5' 8"	Chippendale Polished Ebony	21,780.
IV C	5' 8"	Chippendale Polished Walnut	21,780.
IV C	5' 8"	Chippendale Polished Flame Mahogany	21,780.
III	6' 4"	Polished Ebony	20,580.
III	6' 4"	Polished Walnut	20,580.
III	6' 4"	Polished Flame Mahogany	20,580.
III M	6' 4"	Polished Ebony	29,980
II	7' 9"	Polished Ebony	31,980.
I	9' 3"	Polished Ebony	41,980.

PianoDisc

Note: For "PianoDisc" pianos, see "Knabe".

PDS 128 Plus or PianoCD systems, "factory installed" or retrofitted — prices vary by piano manufacturer or installer, but the following is typical (discounts may apply, especially as incentive to purchase piano):

Playback only	5,300.
Add for Symphony option	1,200.
Add for Record option	1,200.
Add for Powered Speakers, pair, approx.	500.

QRS / Pianomation

Pianomation system, "factory installed" or retrofitted — prices vary by piano manufacturer or installer, but the following is typical (discounts may apply, especially as incentive to purchase piano):

	Pianomation with Orchestration	4,500.
	Add for Record option	900.
Playola system:	Playola "Piano Solo" with carrying case	5,400.
	Playola with Orchestration, speakers, amplifier, and carrying case	6,200.

*For explanation of terms and prices, please see pages 19–24.

Model	Size	Style and Finish	Price*

Rieger-Kloss

Verticals

Model	Size	Style and Finish	Price*
R-109	43"	Continental Polished Ebony	5,300.
R-109	43"	Continental Walnut	5,300.
R-109	43"	Continental Polished Walnut	5,300.
R-109	43"	Continental Polished Mahogany	5,300.
R-109	43"	Continental Oak	5,300.
R-118	47"	Contemporary Polished Ebony	5,580.
R-118	47"	Contemporary Walnut	5,580.
R-118	47"	Contemporary Cherry	5,580.
R-118	47"	Contemporary Oak	5,580.
R-122	48"	Chippendale Polished Ebony	6,710.
R-122	48"	Chippendale Polished Walnut	6,710.
R-122	48"	Chippendale Mahogany	6,710.
R-123	48"	Polished Ebony	6,510.
R-123	48"	Polished Walnut	6,510.
R-123	48"	Polished Mahogany	6,510.
R-125	50"	Polished Ebony (with Renner action)	8,998.
R-126	50"	Polished Ebony	7,190.
R-126	50"	Polished Mahogany	7,190.

Grands

Model	Size	Style and Finish	Price*
R-185	6' 1"	Polished Ebony	21,970.

Sagenhaft

Verticals

Model	Size	Style and Finish	Price*
S-111	44-1/2"	Continental Polished Ebony	2,800.
S-111	44-1/2"	Continental Polished Walnut	2,900.
S-115L	44-1/2"	Polished Ebony	3,200.
S-115L	44-1/2"	Polished Walnut	3,300.
S-121	47"	Polished Ebony	3,720.
S-121	47"	Polished Walnut	3,820.
S-126	50"	Polished Ebony	4,200.
S-126	50"	Polished Walnut	4,300.

Model	Size	Style and Finish	Price*

Samick

Verticals

Model	Size	Style and Finish	Price*
SU-108P	42"	Continental Ebony	3,790.
SU-108P	42"	Continental Polished Ebony	3,790.
SU-108P	42"	Continental Walnut	3,890.
SU-108P	42"	Continental Polished Walnut	3,890.
SU-108P	42"	Continental Polished Mahogany	3,890.
SU-108P	42"	Continental Oak	3,890.
SU-108P	42"	Continental Polished Oak	3,890.
SU-108P	42"	Continental Polished Ivory	3,790.
SU-108P	42"	Continental Polished White	3,790.
SU-143F	43"	French Provincial Cherry	3,990.
SU-143F	43"	French Provincial Oak	3,990.
SU-143M	43"	Mediterranean Oak	3,790.
SU-143MR	43"	Mediterranean Oak	3,890.
SU-143T	43"	Cherry	3,890.
SU-118FA	46-1/2"	Continental Polished Walnut	5,490.
SU-118FA	46-1/2"	Continental Polished Mahogany	5,490.
SU-118H	46-1/2"	Continental Ebony	4,390.
SU-118H	46-1/2"	Continental Polished Ebony	4,390.
SU-118H	46-1/2"	Continental Walnut	4,490.
SU-118H	46-1/2"	Continental Polished Walnut	4,490.
SU-118H	46-1/2"	Continental Mahogany	4,490.
SU-118H	46-1/2"	Continental Polished Mahogany	4,490.
SU-118H	46-1/2"	Continental Polished Ivory	4,390.
SU-147	46-1/2"	Ebony	4,390.
SU-147	46-1/2"	Polished Ebony	4,390.
SU-147	46-1/2"	Walnut	4,390.
SU-147	46-1/2"	Polished Walnut	4,390.
SU-147	46-1/2"	Oak	4,390.
SU-147	46-1/2"	Polished Oak	4,390.
SU-347F	46-1/2"	French Provincial Oak	4,590.
SU-347F	46-1/2"	French Provincial Cherry	4,590.
SU-347M	46-1/2"	Mediterranean Oak	4,390.
SU-347T	46-1/2"	Cherry	4,490.

*For explanation of terms and prices, please see pages 19–24.

Model	Size	Style and Finish	Price*
Samick (continued)			
SU-121B	48"	Ebony	5,060.
SU-121B	48"	Polished Ebony	5,060.
SU-131B	52"	Ebony	5,560.
SU-131B	52"	Polished Ebony	5,560.
Grands			
SG-150	4' 11-1/2"	Ebony	9,200.
SG-150	4' 11-1/2"	Polished Ebony	9,200.
SG-150	4' 11-1/2"	Walnut	9,500.
SG-150	4' 11-1/2"	Polished Walnut	9,500.
SG-150	4' 11-1/2"	Mahogany	9,500.
SG-150	4' 11-1/2"	Polished Mahogany	9,500.
SG-150	4' 11-1/2"	Oak	9,500.
SG-150	4' 11-1/2"	Polished Oak	9,500.
SG-150	4' 11-1/2"	Polished Cherry	9,500.
SG-150	4' 11-1/2"	Polished Ivory	9,200.
SG-150	4' 11-1/2"	Polished White	9,200.
SG-150AF	4' 11-1/2"	French Provincial Ebony	11,050.
SG-150AF	4' 11-1/2"	French Provincial Polished Ebony	11,050.
SG-150AF	4' 11-1/2"	French Provincial Polished Walnut	11,050.
SG-150AF	4' 11-1/2"	French Provincial Mahogany	11,050.
SG-150AF	4' 11-1/2"	French Provincial Polished Mahogany	11,050.
SG-150AF	4' 11-1/2"	French Provincial Oak	11,050.
SG-150KBF	4' 11-1/2"	French Provincial Polished Ebony	11,390.
SG-150KBF	4' 11-1/2"	French Provincial Polished Walnut	11,390.
SG-161	5' 3-1/2"	Ebony	10,700.
SG-161	5' 3-1/2"	Polished Ebony	10,700.
SG-161	5' 3-1/2"	Walnut	11,000.
SG-161	5' 3-1/2"	Polished Walnut	11,000.
SG-161	5' 3-1/2"	Mahogany	11,000.
SG-161	5' 3-1/2"	Polished Mahogany	11,000.
SG-161	5' 3-1/2"	Oak	11,000.
SG-161	5' 3-1/2"	Polished Oak	11,000.
SG-161	5' 3-1/2"	Cherry	11,000.
SG-161	5' 3-1/2"	Polished Ivory	10,700.
SG-161	5' 3-1/2"	French Provincial Polished White	10,700.

Model	Size	Style and Finish	Price*
SG-161KAF	5' 3-1/2"	French Provincial Ebony	13,270.
SG-161KAF	5' 3-1/2"	French Provincial Polished Ebony	13,270.
SG-161KAF	5' 3-1/2"	French Provincial Walnut	13,270.
SG-161KAF	5' 3-1/2"	French Provincial Polished Walnut	13,270.
SG-161KAF	5' 3-1/2"	French Provincial Mahogany	13,270.
SG-161KAF	5' 3-1/2"	French Provincial Polished Mahogany	13,270.
SG-161KAF	5' 3-1/2"	French Provincial Oak	13,270.
SG-161KAF	5' 3-1/2"	French Provincial Polished Oak	13,270.
SG-161KBF	5' 3-1/2"	French Provincial Ebony	13,760.
SG-161KBF	5' 3-1/2"	French Provincial Polished Ebony	13,760.
SG-161KBF	5' 3-1/2"	French Provincial Walnut	13,760.
SG-161KBF	5' 3-1/2"	French Provincial Polished Walnut	13,760.
SG-161KBF	5' 3-1/2"	French Provincial Mahogany	13,760.
SG-161KBF	5' 3-1/2"	French Provincial Polished Mahogany	13,760.
SG-161KBF	5' 3-1/2"	French Provincial Oak	13,760.
SG-161KBF	5' 3-1/2"	French Provincial Polished Oak	13,760.
SG-172	5' 7"	Ebony	11,690.
SG-172	5' 7"	Polished Ebony	11,690.
SG-172	5' 7"	Walnut	11,990.
SG-172	5' 7"	Polished Walnut	11,990.
SG-172	5' 7"	Mahogany	11,990.
SG-172	5' 7"	Polished Mahogany	11,990.
SG-172	5' 7"	Oak	11,990.
SG-172	5' 7"	Polished Oak	11,990.
SG-172	5' 7"	Polished Ivory	11,690.
SG-172	5' 7"	Polished White	11,690.
SG-185	6' 1"	Ebony	12,840.
SG-185	6' 1"	Polished Ebony	12,840.
SG-185	6' 1"	*Walnut*	13,140.
SG-185	6' 1"	*Polished Walnut*	13,140.
SG-185	6' 1"	*Polished Mahogany*	13,140.
SG-185	6' 1"	*Oak*	13,140.
SG-185	6' 1"	*Polished Oak*	13,140.
SG-185	6' 1"	*Polished Ivory*	13,140.
SG-185	6' 1"	*Polished White*	13,140.
WSG-205	6' 8"	Ebony	20,900.
WSG-205	6' 8"	Polished Ebony	20,900.

*For explanation of terms and prices, please see pages 19–24.

Model	Size	Style and Finish	Price*

Samick (continued)

Model	Size	Style and Finish	Price*
WSG-225	7' 4"	Ebony	24,990.
WSG-225	7' 4"	Polished Ebony	24,990.
WSG-275	9' 1"	Polished Ebony	38,900.

Sängler & Söhne / Wieler

Verticals

USC-110	44"	Continental Polished Ebony	2,070.
USC-110	44"	Continental Mahogany	1,990.
USC-110	44"	Continental Polished Mahogany	2,050.
USC-110	44"	Continental Polished White	2,130.
BE-110K	45"	Polished Ebony	2,390.
BE-110K	45"	Polished Mahogany	2,370.
BE-110K	45"	Polished White	2,450.
USC-120	48"	Polished Ebony	2,590.
USC-120	48"	Polished Mahogany	2,570.
USC-120	48"	Polished White	2,650.
USC-120	48"	French Polished Mahogany	2,590.

Schimmel

When not mentioned, satin finish available on special order at same price as high-polish finish.

Verticals

112 E	45"	Empire Polished Mahogany	12,180.
112 S	45"	*Open-pore Oak Ebony*	11,580.
112 S	45"	*Open-pore Walnut*	11,580.
112 S	45"	*Open-pore Oak*	11,580.
114 I	45"	*International Polished Ebony*	11,580.
114 K	45"	*Classicism Polished Ebony*	11,780.
116 S	46"	*Special Polished Ebony*	10,180.
120 I	48"	*International Polished Ebony*	11,780.
120 J	48"	Centennial Polished Mahogany	12,580.
120 LE	48"	Exquisite Polished Ebony	12,380.
120 LE	48"	Exquisite Polished Mahogany	12,580.
120 RC	48"	*Chippendale Polished Ebony*	13,180.

Model	Size	Style and Finish	Price*
120 RC	48"	Chippendale Polished Mahogany	13,380.
120 RI	48"	Intarsia Polished Mahogany	14,380.
120 T	48"	Ebony	12,180.
120 T	48"	Polished Ebony	12,180.
120 T	48"	*Polished Walnut*	12,380.
120 T	48"	Mahogany	12,380.
120 T	48"	Polished Mahogany	12,380.
120 T	48"	*Polished White*	12,580.
120 TN	48"	Noblesse Polished Ebony	12,380.
120 TN	48"	*Noblesse Polished White*	12,780.
122 KE	49"	Exquisite Polished Ebony	12,380.
122 KE	49"	Exquisite Polished Mahogany	12,580.
122 KE	49"	Exquisite Polished Cherry	13,380.
130 T	51"	Ebony	14,180.
130 T	51"	Polished Ebony	14,180.
130 T	51"	*Polished Walnut*	14,380.
130 T	51"	Mahogany	14,380.
130 T	51"	Polished Mahogany	14,380.
130 T	51"	Polished White	14,580.

Grands

Model	Size	Style and Finish	Price*
SC 150 C	5' 1"	Chippendale Polished Mahogany	31,980.
SC 150 C	5' 1"	Chippendale Polished Walnut	31,980.
SC 150 T	5' 1"	Polished Ebony	29,180.
SC 150 T	5' 1"	*Polished Walnut*	29,980.
SC 150 T	5' 1"	*Polished Mahogany*	29,980.
SC 150 T	5' 1"	*Polished White*	30,180.
SP 174 C	5' 10"	*Chippendale Polished Walnut*	33,780.
SP 174 C	5' 10"	*Chippendale Polished Mahogany*	33,780.
SP 174 E	5' 10"	Empire Polished Mahogany	39,180.
SP 174 LE	5' 10"	Limited Edition Polished Ebony	33,980.
SP 174 T	5' 10"	Ebony	30,980.
SP 174 T	5' 10"	Polished Ebony	30,980.
SP 174 T	5' 10"	*Polished Walnut*	31,780.
SP 174 T	5' 10"	Mahogany	31,780.
SP 174 T	5' 10"	Polished Mahogany	31,780.
SP 174 T	5 10"	*Polished White*	31,980.
SP 174 TE	5' 10"	Exquisite Polished Ebony	32,580.

*For explanation of terms and prices, please see pages 19–24.

Model	Size	Style and Finish	Price*

Schimmel (continued)

Model	Size	Style and Finish	Price*
SP 174 TE	5' 10"	Exquisite Polished Mahogany	33,380.
SP 174 TE	5' 10"	Exquisite Intarsia Mahogany	34,580.
SG 174 TJ	5' 10"	Jubilee Polished Ebony	32,980.
SG 174 TJ	5' 10"	Jubilee Polished Mahogany	33,780.
CC 208 C	6' 10"	*Chippendale Polished Walnut*	39,380.
CC 208 C	6' 10"	*Chippendale Polished Mahogany*	39,380.
CC 208 G	6' 10"	*Plexiglass*	81,400.
CC 208 LE	6' 10"	Polished Ebony	39,980.
CC 208 T	6' 10"	Ebony	36,580.
CC 208 T	6' 10"	Polished Ebony	36,580.
CC 208 T	6' 10"	*Polished Walnut*	37,380.
CC 208 T	6' 10"	Mahogany	37,380.
CC 208 T	6' 10"	Polished Mahogany	37,380.
CC 208 T	6' 10"	*Polished White*	37,580.
CO 256 C	8' 4"	Polished Ebony	59,800.

Schirmer & Son

Verticals

Model	Size	Style and Finish	Price*
M-105C	42"	Continental Polished Ebony	4,390.
M-105C	42"	Continental Polished Mahogany	4,390.
M-113CH	44"	Queen Anne Polished Ebony	5,650.
M-113CH	44"	Queen Anne Polished Mahogany	5,650.
M-113CH	44"	Queen Anne Polished Walnut	5,650.
M-113D	44"	Polished Ebony	5,450.
M-113D	44"	Polished Mahogany	5,450.
M-113D	44"	Polished Walnut	5,450.
M-118A	47"	Polished Ebony	5,650.
M-118A	47"	Polished Mahogany	5,650.
M-118A	47"	Polished Walnut	5,650.
M-118A	47"	Oak	5,590.
M-118CH	47"	Chippendale Polished Ebony	5,850.
M-118CH	47"	Chippendale Polished Mahogany	5,850.
M-118CH	47"	Chippendale Polished Walnut	5,850.
M-118CH	47"	Chippendale Polished White	6,250.
M-128E	51"	Polished Ebony	6,450.

Model	Size	Style and Finish	Price*
M-128E	51"	Polished Mahogany	6,450.
Grands			
M-163	5' 4"	Polished Ebony	14,390.
M-190	6' 3"	Polished Ebony	19,190.
M-273	9'	Polished Ebony	37,990.

Schubert

Verticals

Model	Size	Style and Finish	Price
110K	43"	Continental Polished Ebony	2,090.
110K	43"	Continental Polished Mahogany	2,110.
110K	43"	Continental Polished White	2,190.
120K	47"	Polished Ebony	2,190.
120K	47"	Polished Mahogany	2,250.
120K	47"	Brown Ash	2,250.
120K	47"	Hazelnut	2,250.
120K	47"	Oak	2,250.
120K	47"	Polished White	2,290.
120R	47"	Chippendale Polished Ebony	2,390.
120R	47"	Chippendale Polished Mahogany	2,450.
120R	47"	Chippendale Polished White	2,490.

Seiler

Verticals

Model	Size	Style and Finish	Price
116	46"	Continental Polished Ebony	13,848.
116	46"	Continental Open-Pore Walnut	12,744.
116	46"	Continental Open-Pore Oak	12,744.
116	46"	Continental Polished White	14,068.
116	46"	Open-Pore Oak (School)	12,744.
116	46"	Chippendale Open-Pore Walnut	13,220.
116	46"	Mondial Open-Pore Walnut	13,090.
116	46"	Mondial Open-Pore Mahogany	13,090.
116	46"	Mondial Open-Pore Oak	13,090.
116	46"	Mondial Open-Pore Cherry	13,848.
116	46"	Jubilee Polished Ebony	14,056.
116	46"	Jubilee Polished White	14,268.
116	46"	Escorial Open-Pore Cherry Intarsia	14,268.

*For explanation of terms and prices, please see pages 19–24.

Model	Size	Style and Finish	Price*

Seiler (continued)

Model	Size	Style and Finish	Price*
122	48"	Konsole Polished Ebony	14,400.
122	48"	Konsole Open-Pore Walnut	13,448.
122	48"	Konsole Open-Pore Oak	13,448.
122	48'	Konsole Open-Pore Cherry	14,138.
122	48"	Konscle Polished White	14,758.
122	48"	Open-Pore Walnut (School)	12,856.
122	48"	Open-Pore Oak (School)	12,856.
122	48"	Designer Polished Ebony	15,766.
122	48"	Designer Open-Pore Cherry/Macassar	15,766.
122	48"	Vienna Polished Ebony	14,952.
122	48"	Vienna Polished Mahogany with Inlays	16,662.
122	48"	Vienna Polished Walnut with Inlays	16,662.
122	48"	Vienna Open-Pore Cherry Intarsia	15,552.
131	52"	Polished Ebony	15,766.
131	52"	Open-Pore Walnut	14,806.
131	52"	Polished Mahogany	16,248.

Grands

Model	Size	Style and Finish	Price*
180	5' 11"	Polished Ebony	34,468.
180	5' 11"	Open-Pore Walnut	32,468.
180	5' 11"	Polished Walnut	35,420.
180	5' 11"	Open-Pore Mahogany	32,468.
180	5' 11"	Polished Mahogany	35,420.
180	5' 11"	Polished White	34,944.
180	5' 11"	Chippendale Open-Pore Walnut	34,994.
180	5' 11"	Westminster Polished Mahogany Intarsia	46,380.
180	5' 11"	Florenz Polished Walnut/Myrtle Intarsia	46,380.
180	5' 11"	Florenz Polished Mahogany/Myrtle Intar	46,380.
180	5' 11"	Louvre Polished Ebony	37,104.
180	5' 11"	Louvre Polished White	37,572.
180	5' 11"	Louvre Polished Cherry Intarsia	46,380.
180	5' 11"	Showmaster Chrome/Brass/Polyester	103,668.
206	6' 9"	Polished Ebony	38,510.
240	8'	Polished Ebony	53,406.

Steinway & Sons

Verticals

Model	Size	Style and Finish	Price*
4510	45"	Sheraton Ebony	13,500.
4510	45"	Sheraton Mahogany	14,000.
4510	45"	Sheraton Walnut	14,600.
4510	45"	*Add for high-polish finish*	2,500.
4510	45"	140th Anniversary Mahogany	14,700.
1098	46-1/2"	Ebony	12,400.
1098	46-1/2"	Mahogany	12,900.
1098	46-1/2"	Walnut	13,500.
1098	46-1/2"	*Add for high-polish finish*	2,500.
K-52	52"	Ebony	16,500.
K-52	52"	Mahogany	17,600.
K-52	52"	Walnut	18,200.
K-52	52"	*Add for high-polish finish*	3,300.

Grands

Note: Crown Jewel Collection models (†) are being produced with a "Satin Lustre" finish, which is between satin and high-polish in glossiness. Other models can be special-ordered with this new finish at an extra charge, which varies by model.

Model	Size	Style and Finish	Price*
S	5' 1"	Ebony	27,600.
S	5' 1"	Mahogany	30,100.
S	5' 1"	Walnut	31,200.
S	5' 1"	*Add for high-polish finish*	4,200.
S	5' 1"	*†Figured Sapele*	34,100.
S	5' 1"	*†Kewazinga Bubinga*	34,800.
S	5' 1"	*†East Indian Rosewood*	38,500.
S	5' 1"	*†Santos Rosewood*	38,900.
S	5' 1"	*†Macassar*	40,600.
S	5' 1"	*†Hepplewhite Dark Cherry*	36,300.
M	5' 7"	Ebony	31,900.
M	5' 7"	Mahogany	34,600.
M	5' 7"	Walnut	35,700.
M	5' 7"	*Add for high-polish finish*	5,100.
M	5' 7"	*†Figured Sapele*	38,400.
M	5' 7"	*†Kewazinga Bubinga*	39,400.

*For explanation of terms and prices, please see pages 19–24.

Model	Size	Style and Finish	Price*

Steinway & Sons (continued)

Model	Size	Style and Finish	Price*
M	5' 7"	*†East Indian Rosewood*	43,400.
M	5' 7"	*†Santos Rosewood*	43,800.
M	5' 7"	*†Macassar*	45,800.
M	5' 7"	*†Hepplewhite Dark Cherry*	41,500.
M SK-1014	5' 7"	Chippendale Mahogany	43,400.
M SK-1014	5' 7"	Chippendale Walnut	44,600.
M SK-501	5' 7"	LXV Walnut	57,400.
L	5' 10-1/2"	Ebony	36,100.
L	5' 10-1/2"	Mahogany	38,800.
L	5' 10-1/2"	Walnut	40,500.
L	5' 10-1/2"	*Add for high-polish finish*	5,700.
L	5' 10-1/2"	"Instrument of the Immortals" Ebony	43,200.
L	5' 10-1/2"	"Instrument of the Immortals" Rosewood	53,500.
L	5' 10-1/2"	*†Figured Sapele*	43,300.
L	5' 10-1/2"	*†Kewazinga Bubinga*	44,500.
L	5' 10-1/2"	*†East Indian Rosewood*	49,400.
L	5' 10-1/2"	*†Santos Rosewood*	49,500.
L	5' 10-1/2"	*†Macassar*	51,900.
L	5' 10-1/2"	*†Hepplewhite Dark Cherry*	46,700.
B	6' 10-1/2"	Ebony	46,900.
B	6' 10-1/2"	Mahogany	50,100.
B	6' 10-1/2"	Walnut	51,800.
B	6' 10-1/2"	*Add for high-polish finish*	7,000.
B	6' 10-1/2"	"Instrument of the Immortals" Ebony	55,300.
B	6' 10-1/2"	"Instrument of the Immortals" Rosewood	68,500.
B	6' 10-1/2"	*†Figured Sapele*	55,300.
B	6' 10-1/2"	*†Kewazinga Bubinga*	57,100.
B	6' 10-1/2"	*†East Indian Rosewood*	63,000.
B	6' 10-1/2"	*†Santos Rosewood*	63,600.
B	6' 10-1/2"	*†Macassar*	66,400.
B	6' 10-1/2"	*†Hepplewhite Dark Cherry*	60,000.
D	8' 11-3/4"	Ebony	71,900.
D	8' 11-3/4"	Walnut	79,200.
D	8' 11-3/4"	*Add for high-polish finish*	9,900.
D	8' 11-3/4"	*†Figured Sapele*	85,400.
D	8' 11-3/4"	*†Kewazinga Bubinga*	87,800.

Model	Size	Style and Finish	Price*
D	8' 11-3/4"	†*East Indian Rosewood*	96,600.
D	8' 11-3/4"	†*Santos Rosewood*	97,200.
D	8' 11-3/4"	†*Macassar*	101,200.
D	8' 11-3/4"	†*Hepplewhite Dark Cherry*	92,900.

Story & Clark

Verticals

3311	42"	Oak	3,790.
3312	42"	Cherry	3,790.
3313	42"	Walnut	3,790.
3314	42"	Southwest Bleached Oak	3,790.
1111	44"	Polished Ebony	2,590.
1112	44"	Polished Mahogany	2,590.
1113	44"	Walnut	2,590.
1114	44"	French Provincial Cherry	3,190.
1115	44"	American Oak	3,190.
4411	46"	Church Oak	4,390.
4412	46"	Oak (School)	4,390.

Grands

SC407	4' 7"	Polished Ebony with Pianomation	14,740.
SC501	5' 1"	Polished Ebony with Pianomation	15,910.
54	5' 4"	Ebony	12,000.
54	5' 4"	Polished Ebony	12,000.
55	5' 5"	Ebony	19,600.
55	5' 5"	Cherry	19,600.

Walter, Charles R.

Verticals

1520	43"	Oak	6,466.
1520	43"	Cherry	6,686.
1520	43"	Walnut	6,716.
1520	43"	Mahogany	6,818.
1520	43"	Mediterranean Oak	6,444.
1520	43"	Italian Provincial Oak	6,470.
1520	43"	Italian Provincial Walnut	6,718.
1520	43"	French Provincial Oak	6,710.

*For explanation of terms and prices, please see pages 19–24.

Model	Size	Style and Finish	Price*

Walter, Charles R. (continued)

Model	Size	Style and Finish	Price*
1520	43"	French Provincial Walnut	6,908.
1520	43"	French Provincial Cherry	6,910.
1520	43"	Country Classic Oak	6,498.
1520	43"	Country Classic Cherry	6,638.
1520	43"	Queen Anne Oak	6,780.
1520	43"	Queen Anne Cherry	6,970.
1520	43"	Queen Anne Mahogany	6,974.
1500	45"	Ebony	6,290.
1500	45"	Polished Ebony	6,592.
1500	45"	Oak	6,042.
1500	45"	Walnut	6,288.
1500	45"	Mahogany	6,390.
1500	45"	Gothic Oak	6,404.

Grands

Model	Size	Style and Finish	Price*
W190	6' 3"	Ebony	27,800.
W190	6' 3"	Mahogany	29,200.
W190	6' 3"	Walnut	29,200.

Weber

Verticals

Model	Size	Style and Finish	Price*
W-40	42"	85-note Continental Polished Ebony	4,100.
W-41A	43"	Continental Polished Ebony	4,200.
W-41A	43"	Continental Walnut	4,460.
W-41A	43"	Continental Polished Walnut	4,460.
W-41A	43"	Continental Polished Mahogany	4,460.
W-41A	43"	Continental Polished Brown Mahogany	4,460.
W-41A	43"	Continental Polished Ivory	4,240.
W-41A	43"	Continental Polished White	4,240.
WF-41	43"	Cherry	4,600.
WF-41	43"	Mediterranean Oak	4,700.
WF-41	43"	French Provincial Cherry	4,700.
WFX-43	43-1/2"	French Cherry	5,120.
WFD-44	44-1/2"	Mahogany	5,500.
WFD-44	44-1/2"	Oak	5,500.
WFD-44	44-1/2"	French Provincial Cherry	5,500.

Model	Size	Style and Finish	Price*
W-45C	45"	Chippendale Polished Mahogany	5,780.
WC-46	46"	Continental Polished Ebony	5,180.
WC-46	46"	Continental Polished Mahogany	5,320.
WC-46	46"	Continental Polished Walnut	5,320.
WC-46	46"	American Oak	5,180.
WC-46	46"	American Walnut	5,180.
W-48	48"	Ebony	5,800.
W-48	48"	Polished Ebony	5,800.
W-48	48"	Walnut	6,060.
W-48	48"	Polished Walnut	6,060.
W-48	48"	Polished Mahogany	6,060.
W-48	48"	Polished Brown Mahogany	6,060.
W-53	52"	Polished Ebony	6,600.
W-53	52"	Polished Mahogany	6,880.
Grands			
WG-50	4' 11"	Ebony	11,180.
WG-50	4' 11"	Polished Ebony	11,180.
WG-50	4' 11"	Walnut	11,920.
WG-50	4' 11"	Polished Mahogany	11,920.
WG-50	4' 11"	Polished Brown Mahogany	11,920.
WG-50	4' 11"	Polished Ivory	11,580.
WG-50	4' 11"	Polished White	11,580.
WG-50	4' 11"	Queen Anne Polished Ebony	13,120.
WG-50	4' 11"	Queen Anne Polished Mahogany	13,620.
WG-50	4' 11"	Queen Anne Polished Brown Mahogany	13,620.
WG-50	4' 11"	Queen Anne Cherry	13,780.
WG-50	4' 11"	Queen Anne Polished White	13,620.
WG-51	5' 1"	Ebony	12,200.
WG-51	5' 1"	Polished Ebony	12,200.
WG-51	5' 1"	Walnut	12,740.
WG-51	5' 1"	Polished Walnut	12,740.
WG-51	5' 1"	Polished Mahogany	12,740.
WG-51	5' 1"	Polished Brown Mahogany	12,740.
WG-51	5' 1"	Polished Ivory	12,640.
WG-51	5' 1"	Polished White	12,640.
WG-57	5' 7"	Ebony	14,260.
WG-57	5' 7"	Polished Ebony	14,260.

*For explanation of terms and prices, please see pages 19–24.

Model	Size	Style and Finish	Price*

Weber (continued)

Model	Size	Style and Finish	Price*
WG-57	5' 7"	Walnut	14,860.
WG-57	5' 7"	Polished Walnut	14,860.
WG-57	5' 7"	Polished Mahogany	14,860.
WG-57	5' 7"	Polished Brown Mahogany	14,860.
WG-57	5' 7"	Polished Ivory	14,660.
WG-57	5' 7"	Polished White	14,660.
WG-60	6' 1"	Ebony	15,160.
WG-60	6' 1"	Polished Ebony	15,160.
WG-60	6' 1"	Polished Ivory	15,760.
WG-70	7'	Ebony	23,500.
WG-70	7'	Polished Ebony	23,500.
WG-90	9'	Ebony	46,760.
WG-90	9'	Polished Ebony	46,760.

Weinbach

Verticals

Model	Size	Style and Finish	Price*
104-III	42"	Continental Polished Ebony	4,700.
104-III	42"	Continental Polished Walnut	4,700.
104-III	42"	Continental Polished Flame Mahogany	4,700.
114-I	45"	Chippendale Polished Walnut	5,500.
114-I	45"	Chippendale Polished Flame Mahogany	5,500.
114-IC	45"	Chippendale Polished Walnut	5,780.
114-IC	45"	Chippendale Polished Flame Mahogany	5,780.
114-II	45"	Polished Ebony	4,780.
114-II	45"	Polished Walnut	4,780.
114-II	45"	Polished Flame Mahogany	4,780.
114-IV	45"	Polished Ebony	5,180.
114-IV	45"	Polished Walnut	5,180.
114-IV	45"	Polished Flame Mahogany	5,180.
124-II	50"	Polished Ebony	5,980.
124-II	50"	Polished Walnut	5,980.
124-II	50"	Polished Flame Mahogany	5,980.

Grands

Model	Size	Style and Finish	Price*
155	5' 3"	Polished Ebony	15,180.
155	5' 3"	Polished Walnut	15,180.

Model	Size	Style and Finish	Price*
155	5' 3"	Polished Flame Mahogany	15,180.
170	5' 8"	Polished Ebony	16,380.
170	5' 8"	Polished Walnut	16,380.
170	5' 8"	Polished Flame Mahogany	16,380.
192	6' 4"	Polished Ebony	18,980.
192	6' 4"	Polished Walnut	18,980.
192	6' 4"	Polished Flame Mahogany	18,980.

Wurlitzer

Verticals

1175	37"	Country Oak	3,180.
1176	37"	Queen Anne Cherry	3,180.
2270	42"	Ribbon-Striped Mahogany	3,590.
2275	42"	Country Oak	3,590.
2276	42"	Queen Anne Cherry	3,590.

Grands

C143	4' 7"	Ebony	9,460.
C143	4' 7"	Polished Ebony	9,460.
C143	4' 7"	Polished Mahogany	9,900.
C143	4' 7"	Polished Oak	9,900.
C143	4' 7"	Polished White	9,460.
C153	5' 1"	Ebony	10,820.
C153	5' 1"	Polished Ebony	10,820.
C153	5' 1"	Polished Mahogany	11,320.
C153	5' 1"	Walnut	11,320.
C153	5' 1"	Oak	11,320.
C153	5' 1"	Polished Ivory	10,820.
C153QA	5' 1"	Queen Anne Polished Mahogany	12,760.
C153QA	5' 1"	Queen Anne Oak	12,760.
C153QA	5' 1"	Queen Anne Cherry	12,760.
C173	5' 8"	Ebony	12,184.
C173	5' 8"	Polished Ebony	12,184.
C173	5' 8"	Polished Mahogany	12,700.
C173	5' 8"	Polished White	12,184.

*For explanation of terms and prices, please see pages 19–24.

Model	Size	Style and Finish	Price*

Yamaha

Acoustic Verticals

Model	Size	Style and Finish	Price*
M1F	44"	Continental Ebony	5,390.
M1F	44"	Continental Polished Ebony	5,490.
M1F	44"	Continental American Walnut	5,590.
M1F	44"	Continental Polished American Walnut	6,790.
M1F	44"	Continental Polished Mahogany	6,790.
M1F	44"	Continental Light American Oak	5,590.
M1F	44"	Continental Polished White	6,690.
M1F	44"	Continental Polished Ivory	6,690.
M500C	44"	Cottage Cherry	4,590.
M500CM	44"	Country Manor Light Oak	5,890.
M500CV	44"	Country Villa White Oak	6,090.
M500F	44"	Florentine Light Oak	4,590.
M500G	44"	Georgian Mahogany	5,490.
M500H	44"	Hancock Brown Cherry	4,390.
M500M	44"	Milano Dark Oak	4,590.
M500P	44"	Parisian Cherry	5,690.
M500QA	44"	Queen Anne Cherry	4,790.
M500S	44"	Sheraton Mahogany	4,390.
P22T	45"	American Walnut	4,790.
P22T	45"	Black Oak	4,790.
P22T	45"	Dark Oak	4,790.
P22T	45"	Light Oak	4,790.
P2E	45"	Continental Ebony	5,890.
P2E	45"	Continental Polished Ebony	5,890.
P2E	45"	Continental American Walnut	5,990.
P2E	45"	Continental Polished American Walnut	6,990.
P2E	45"	Continental Polished Mahogany	6,990.
P2E	45"	Continental Light American Oak	5,890.
P2E	45"	Continental Polished White	6,890.
U1S	48"	Ebony	7,190.
U1S	48"	Polished Ebony	7,290.
U1S	48"	American Walnut	7,590.
U1S	48"	Polished American Walnut	8,190.
U1S	48"	Polished Mahogany	8,190.
WX1S	48"	Polished Ebony	9,490.

Model	Size	Style and Finish	Price*
WX1S	48"	American Walnut	9,690.
U3S	52"	Polished Ebony	9,690.
U3S	52"	Polished American Walnut	10,390.
U3S	52"	Polished Mahogany	10,790.
WX7S	52"	Polished Ebony	12,990.
WX7S	52"	American Walnut	13,190.

Disklavier Verticals

Model	Size	Style and Finish	Price*
MX80A	44"	Continental Polished Ebony	9,466.
MX80A	44"	Continental American Walnut	9,390.
MX80A	44"	Continental Polished Mahogany	10,590.
MX80A	44"	Continental Polished Ivory	10,490.
MX80A	44"	Continental Polished White	10,490.
MX85CM	44"	Country Manor Light Oak	9,990.
MX85CV	44"	Country Villa White Oak	10,190.
MX85G	44"	Georgian Mahogany	9,590.
MX85P	44"	Parisian Cherry	9,790.
MX85QA	44"	Queen Anne Cherry	8,890.
MX88	45"	Walnut	9,286.
MX88	45"	Black Oak	9,286.
MX88	45"	Light Oak	9,286.
MX100II	48"	Polished Ebony	12,890.
MX100II	48"	American Walnut	13,218.
MX100II	48"	Polished White	13,080.

Silent Verticals

Model	Size	Style and Finish	Price*
MP50C	44"	Cottage Cherry	6,790.
MP50CM	44"	Country Manor Light Oak	8,258.
MP50CV	44"	Country Villa White Oak	8,470.
MP50F	44"	Florentine Light Oak	6,790.
MP50G	44"	Georgian Mahogany	7,834.
MP50H	44"	Hancock Brown Cherry	6,590.
MP50M	44"	Milano Dark Oak	6,790.
MP50P	44"	Parisian Cherry	8,046.
MP50QA	44"	Queen Anne Cherry	6,990.
MP50S	44"	Sheraton Mahogany	6,590.
MP51 PE	44"	Continental Polished Ebony	7,690.
MP100 PE	48"	Polished Ebony	9,424.

*For explanation of terms and prices, please see pages 19–24.

Model	Size	Style and Finish	Price*

Yamaha (continued)

Silent Disklavier Verticals

Model	Size	Style and Finish	Price*
MPX100II	48"	Polished Ebony	13,954.
MPX100II	48"	American Walnut	14,492.
MPX100II	48"	Polished White	14,314.

Acoustic Grands

Model	Size	Style and Finish	Price*
GH1B	5' 3"	Ebony	12,990.
GH1B	5' 3"	Polished Ebony	13,290.
GH1B	5' 3"	American Walnut	14,790.
GH1B	5' 3"	Polished American Walnut	14,790.
GH1B	5' 3"	Polished Mahogany	14,790.
GH1B	5' 3"	Polished Ivory	14,790.
GH1B	5' 3"	Polished White	14,390.
C1	5' 3"	Ebony	16,790.
C1	5' 3"	Polished Ebony	17,090.
C1	5' 3"	American Walnut	19,290.
C1	5' 3"	Polished Walnut	20,790.
C1	5' 3"	Polished Mahogany	19,990.
C1	5' 3"	Polished Ivory	19,790.
C1	5' 3"	Polished White	19,290.
C2	5' 8"	Ebony	19,090.
C2	5' 8"	Polished Ebony	19,390.
C2	5' 8"	American Walnut	21,990.
C2	5' 8"	Polished Walnut	22,690.
C2	5' 8"	Polished Mahogany	21,990.
C2	5' 8"	Polished Rosewood	28,090.
C2	5' 8"	Polished Ivory	21,290.
C2	5' 8"	Polished White	20,790.
C3	6' 1"	Ebony	26,190.
C3	6' 1"	Polished Ebony	26,390.
C3	6' 1"	American Walnut	28,990.
C3	6' 1"	Polished Mahogany	29,390.
C3	6' 1"	Polished White	26,990.
S4	6' 3"	Polished Ebony	47,390.
C5	6' 7"	Ebony	28,290.
C5	6' 7"	Polished Ebony	28,490.

Model	Size	Style and Finish	Price*
C5	6' 7"	American Walnut	31,190.
C6	6' 11"	Ebony	31,390.
C6	6' 11"	Polished Ebony	31,590.
S6	6' 11"	Polished Ebony	53,590.
C7	7' 6"	Ebony	35,790.
C7	7' 6"	Polished Ebony	35,990.
CFIIIS	9'	Polished Ebony	97,990.

Disklavier Grands

Model	Size	Style and Finish	Price*
DA1 II	4' 11"	Polished Ebony	24,030.
DGH1BII	5' 3"	*Ebony*	23,990.
DGH1BII	5' 3"	Polished Ebony	24,290.
DGH1BXG	5' 3"	Polished Ebony — playback only	20,760.
DGH1BII	5' 3"	American Walnut	25,790.
DGH1BII	5' 3"	*Polished American Walnut*	28,716.
DGH1BII	5' 3"	*Polished Mahogany*	28,716.
DGH1BII	5' 3"	*Polished Ivory*	27,420.
DGH1BII	5' 3"	Polished White	25,868.
DC1 II	5' 3"	*Ebony*	28,276.
DC1 II	5' 3"	Polished Ebony	28,560.
DC1 II	5' 3"	American Walnut	31,422.
DC1 II	5' 3"	*Polished American Walnut*	33,414.
DC1 II	5' 3"	*Polished Mahogany*	32,844.
DC1 II	5' 3"	*Polished Ivory*	31,136.
DC1 II	5' 3"	Polished White	30,568.
DC2 II	5' 8"	*Ebony*	30,290.
DC2 II	5' 8"	Polished Ebony	30,852.
DC2 II	5' 8"	American Walnut	33,190.
DC2 II	5' 8"	*Polished American Walnut*	33,890.
DC2 II	5' 8"	*Polished Mahogany*	33,388.
DC2 II	5' 8"	*Polished Ivory*	32,490.
DC2 II	5' 8"	Polished White	31,988.
DC3 II	6' 1"	*Ebony*	37,396.
DC3 II	6' 1"	Polished Ebony	37,590.
DC3 II	6' 1"	American Walnut	40,590.
DC3 II	6' 1"	*Polished Mahogany*	39,790.
DC3 II	6' 1"	Polished White	38,190.
DS4 II	6' 3"	Polished Ebony	59,390.

*For explanation of terms and prices, please see pages 19–24.

Model	Size	Style and Finish	Price*

Yamaha (continued)

Model	Size	Style and Finish	Price*
DC5 II	6' 7"	Ebony	39,690.
DC5 II	6' 7"	Polished Ebony	39,890.
DC6 II	6' 11"	Ebony	42,790.
DC6 II	6' 11"	Polished Ebony	42,918.
DS6 II	6' 11"	Polished Ebony	65,590.
DC7 II	7' 6"	Ebony	47,190.
DC7 II	7' 6"	Polished Ebony	47,390.
DCFIIIS-II	9'	Polished Ebony	109,990.

Silent Grands

Model	Size	Style and Finish	Price*
A1S PE	4' 11"	Polished Ebony	20,064.
C1S PE	5' 3"	Polished Ebony	21,794.
C2S PE	5' 8"	Polished Ebony	24,084.
C3S PE	6' 1"	Polished Ebony	31,058.

Young Chang

Verticals

Model	Size	Style and Finish	Price*
U-107A	42"	Continental Ebony	5,100.
U-107A	42"	Continental Polished Ebony	5,100.
U-107A	42"	Continental Walnut	5,280.
U-107A	42"	Continental Polished Walnut	5,280.
U-107A	42"	Continental Polished Red Mahogany	5,280.
U-107A	42"	Continental Polished Oak	5,280.
U-107A	42"	Continental Polished Ivory	5,240.
U-107A	42"	Continental Polished White	5,240.
E-101	43"	Continental Polished Ebony	4,100.
E-101	43"	Continental Polished Walnut	4,360.
E-101	43"	Continental Polished Oak	4,360.
E-101	43"	Continental Polished Ivory	4,140.
E-101	43"	Continental Polished White	4,140.
E-102	43"	Continental Polished Ebony	4,200.
E-102	43"	Continental Polished Walnut	4,460.
E-102	43"	Continental Polished Red Mahogany	4,460.
E-102	43"	Continental Polished Brown Mahogany	4,460.
E-102	43"	Continental Polished Oak	4,460.
E-102	43"	Continental Polished Ivory	4,240.

Model	Size	Style and Finish	Price*
E-102	43"	Continental Polished White	4,240.
U-109C	43"	Queen Anne Polished Ebony	5,300.
U-109C	43"	Queen Anne Polished Walnut	5,460.
U-109C	43"	Queen Anne Polished Red Mahogany	5,460.
F-108B	43-1/2"	Mahogany	4,940.
F-108B	43-1/2"	Italian Provincial Walnut	4,940.
F-108B	43-1/2"	Mediterranean Oak	4,940.
F-108B	43-1/2"	Queen Anne Oak	4,960.
F-108B	43-1/2"	French Provincial Cherry	5,120.
F-108B	43-1/2"	Queen Anne Cherry	5,120.
F-116	46-1/2"	Mediterranean Oak	5,600.
F-116	46-1/2"	Italian Provincial Walnut	5,600.
F-116	46-1/2"	French Provincial Cherry	5,740.
U-116	46-1/2"	Ebony	5,180.
U-116	46-1/2"	Polished Ebony	5,180.
U-116	46-1/2"	American Walnut	5,320.
U-116	46-1/2"	American Oak	5,320.
U-116	46-1/2"	Polished Oak	5,320.
U-116S	46-1/2"	American Walnut	5,180.
U-116S	46-1/2"	American Oak	5,180.
U-121	48"	Ebony	5,860.
U-121	48"	Polished Ebony	5,860.
U-121	48"	Walnut	6,120.
U-121	48"	Polished Walnut	6,120.
U-121	48"	American Oak	6,120.
U-121	48"	Polished Oak	6,120.
U-121	48"	Polished Brown Mahogany	6,120.
U-131	52"	Ebony	6,600.
U-131	52"	Polished Ebony	6,600.
U-131	52"	Walnut	6,880.
U-131	52"	Polished Walnut	6,880.
Grands			
G-150	4' 11-1/2"	Ebony	11,180.
G-150	4' 11-1/2"	Polished Ebony	11,180.
G-150	4' 11-1/2"	American Walnut	11,900.
G-150	4' 11-1/2"	Polished Red Mahogany	11,920.
G-150	4' 11-1/2"	Polished Brown Mahogany	11,920.

*For explanation of terms and prices, please see pages 19–24.

Model	Size	Style and Finish	Price*

Young Chang (continued)

Model	Size	Style and Finish	Price*
G-150	4' 11-1/2"	Polished Oak	11,920.
G-150	4' 11-1/2"	Polished Ivory	11,580.
G-150	4' 11-1/2"	Polished White	11,580.
G-150	4' 11-1/2"	Queen Anne Polished Ebony	13,120.
G-150	4' 11-1/2"	Queen Anne Polished Red Mahog.	13,620.
G-150	4' 11-1/2"	Queen Anne Polished Oak	13,620.
G-150	4' 11-1/2"	Queen Anne Cherry	13,780.
G-150	4' 11-1/2"	Queen Anne Polished Ivory	13,360.
G-150	4' 11-1/2"	Queen Anne Polished White	13,360.
G-157	5' 2"	Ebony	12,360.
G-157	5' 2"	Polished Ebony	12,360.
G-157	5' 2"	Walnut	12,860.
G-157	5' 2"	Polished Walnut	12,860.
G-157	5' 2"	Polished Red Mahogany	12,860.
G-157	5' 2"	Polished Brown Mahogany	12,860.
G-157	5' 2"	Polished Oak	12,860.
G-157	5' 2"	Polished Ivory	12,720.
G-157	5' 2"	Polished White	12,720.
G-157D	5' 2"	Country French Oak	15,640.
G-157D	5' 2"	Country French Cherry	15,940.
G-157D	5' 2"	Queen Anne Red Mahogany	15,640.
G-157D	5' 2"	Queen Anne Cherry	15,940.
G-175	5' 9"	Ebony	14,560.
G-175	5' 9"	Polished Ebony	14,560.
G-175	5' 9"	Walnut	15,160.
G-175	5' 9"	Polished Walnut	15,160.
G-175	5' 9"	Polished Red Mahogany	15,160.
G-175	5' 9"	Polished Brown Mahogany	15,160.
G-175	5' 9"	Polished Oak	15,160.
G-175	5' 9"	Polished Ivory	14,960.
G-175	5' 9"	Polished White	14,960.
G-175D	5' 9"	Empire Polished Brown Mahogany	17,640.
G-185	6' 1"	Ebony	15,160.
G-185	6' 1"	Polished Ebony	15,160.
G-185	6' 1"	Walnut	15,840.
G-185	6' 1"	Polished Walnut	15,840.

Model	Size	Style and Finish	Price*
G-185	6' 1"	Polished Red Mahogany	15,840.
G-185	6' 1"	Polished Brown Mahogany	15,840.
G-185	6' 1"	Polished Ivory	15,760.
G-208	6' 10"	Polished Ebony	19,180.
G-213	7'	Ebony	23,500.
G-213	7'	Polished Ebony	23,500.
G-275	9'	Ebony	46,760.
G-275	9'	Polished Ebony	46,760.

*For explanation of terms and prices, please see pages 19–24.

- *Candid brand-by-brand reviews of new pianos*

- *Sales gimmicks to watch out for — and the real differences in piano quality and features*

- *How to negotiate the best deal*

- *Tips on finding, inspecting, appraising, and buying a used piano*

- *Special section on buying an older Steinway*

- *Piano moving, storage, tuning, servicing*

800-545-2022 • 617-522-7182
fax: 617-524-2172 • e-mail: pianobk@tiac.net
world wide web: http://www.tiac.net/users/pianobk
**BROOKSIDE PRESS • P.O. BOX 178
JAMAICA PLAIN, MA 02130**

THE PIANO BOOK

BUYING & OWNING A NEW OR USED PIANO

LARRY FINE

FOREWORD BY KEITH JARRETT

THIRD EDITION
REVISED & UPDATED

194 pages • 8-1/2 x 11 • 100 line drawings
Hardcover $26.95 • Paperback $16.95
Shipping/handling $2.50 ($3.50 foreign)